About the Author

William M. Foster received his engineering degree from the University of California at Los Angeles. He is manager of Solar Energy Markets for Alcoa and is active in several trade associations as a solar advisor.

No. 906
$7.95

Homeowner's Guide
to Solar
Heating & Cooling

By William M. Foster

TAB BOOKS
Blue Ridge Summit, Pa. 17214

FIRST EDITION

FIRST PRINTING—SEPTEMBER 1976

Copyright © 1976 by TAB BOOKS

Printed in the United States
of America

Hardbound Edition: International Standard Book No. 0-8306-6906-X

Paperbound Edition: International Standard Book No. 0-8306-5906-4

Library of Congress Card Number: 76-24786

Cover photo courtesy Jerry Sarapochiello.

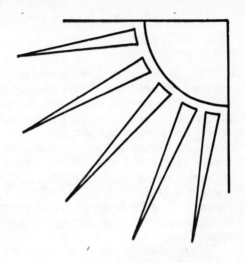

Preface

Use of the sun in home heating applications isn't new—as far back as 1949 there were more than 30,000 solar heating systems in the city of Miami alone! But as natural gas became available and electricity rates dropped, the solar-energy market declined. Why pay more for energy from the sun when there are abundant sources beneath our feet? Ultimately, we were to learn that energy from the ground is not available in unlimited quantities. But as long as oil could be obtained in boundless supply from friendly nations at a cost that kept earth resources cheaper then extraterrestrial energy sources, it was inevitable that solar energy conversion would remain unattractive as a practical alternative.

In the fall of 1973 the oil embargo sent shock waves through our economy and put an end to decades of low-cost power. We began to look elsewhere for potentially practical sources of energy—sources with promise of dependability, economy, and efficiency. Solar energy drew renewed attention from interested and concerned scientists and politicians throughout the world.

Where sunlight abounds, solar water heaters are competitive today. And in locations where electricity costs more than 3½ ¢ per kilowatt-hour and room heating is required for appreciable portions of the year, solar heating is cheaper, more trouble-free, and measurably more dependable than any of the commercial alternatives.

Of course, comparisons become meaningless if alternative fuels are not available. When coffee prices were going through their soaring upward spiral, one shopper complained to her grocer at the checkout stand that a competing market was advertising a major brand at little more than a dollar a pound. Seeing the woman with an armload of one-pound tins that were nearly double that price, the grocer asked why she hadn't stopped at his competitor's instead. She had, she said, but their supplies were exhausted. To which the grocer replied, "When *I* run out, I'll cut the price to two pounds for a dollar!" There are numerous places in this country where solar energy is the only show in town.

Many communities have taken a protective and conservative stand with their power disbursement. There are reports of homes that were denied natural-gas connections. And in state after state, use of available fuel for such functions as swimming-pool heating has been declared frivolous or deemed a low-priority luxury. In such applications solar energy may very soon become the sole remaining option.

As a homeowner, you must make your own decision as to whether or not the time is right and ripe for you to invest in a solar system. This book will serve as a useful tool in making that decision, for it provides you with a step-by-step analysis of the question, with a clear course of action set by the first chapter.

William M. Foster

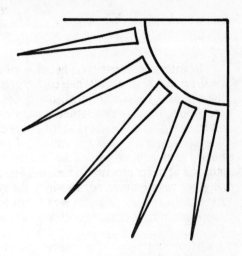

Contents

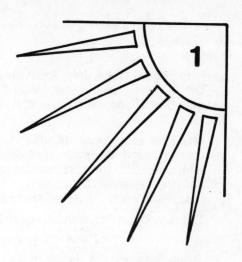

Is Solar Heating Economical?

Based on today's technology and low volume of production, a solar room heating system will cost several thousand dollars to purchase and install. The most frequently quoted prices range from $4000 to $8000. Before seriously considering one of these units, you should calculate your current annual heating bill. If it exceeds $500, a solar heating system may make economic sense. With an annual bill less than this amount, it is of questionable value at present commercial prices.

To calculate the energy used by your family for room heating, fill in your home's fuel consumption using one of the following formulas, depending on whether you use electricity, natural gas, or heating oil.

The rationale for the formulas isn't the least bit difficult. You start by jotting down the total power-consumption figure for a given year, then subtract the amount used for functions other than heating. Multiply this figure by a conversion factor to give you a figure that represents an accurate accounting of the annual heat-energy requirement for your home in one year.

In case you're wondering how to determine the amount of other-than-heating fuel consumption, which must be subtracted from the total, follow these guidelines. Take the total fuel use for that quarter of the year when heating is least

likely to be used (June, July, and August) and multiply it by 4
to get a close approximation of a year's nonheating
consumption. If you use electric heat, the calculation will go
like this:

total year's fuel consumption (F_T), in kilowatt-hours
− consumption during summer multiplied by 4 ($F_S \times 4$)
= total nonheating fuel consumption (F_N), kilowatt-hours
× 3413 (the conversion factor, k)
= annual heat energy in British thermal units (e_H)

Expressed as a conventional equation:

$$e_H = F_T - 4F_S \times k$$

Regardless of the units involved—kilowatt-hours for
electricity, cubic feet or therms for natural gas, gallons for
oil—the equation remains the same except for the conversion
factor, which converts the actual unit of measure into British
thermal units, the common denominator for comparing the
various approaches.

For natural gas, in which the unit of measure is the cubic
foot, the conversion factor k to use is 1035 (rather than 3413);
for therms the conversion factor is 100,000. For fuel oil, with
gallons as the basic unit of measure, k is 140,000. And, as a
means of comparison, the conversion factor for coal is 13,500,
for steam, 1.2.

Let's perform an example calculation for a well insulated
two-story home located in Pittsburgh and using natural gas as
heating fuel. The year's monthly fuel-consumption figures are

Table 1-1. Monthly Fuel Consumption

Month	Quantity, cu ft	Fuel Cost
January	21,200	$ 27.47
February	15,500	21.55
March	18,000	24.81
April	8,500	13.28
May	4,000	7.81
June	3,100	7.00
July	3,000	6.93
August	3,100	7.18
September	6,100	11.70
October	7,100	13.12
November	20,000	31.44
December	19,200	30.58
Total	128,800	$202.87

Table 1-2. Annual Water-Heating Fuel Consumption

Month	Quantity	Amount
June	3.1	$ 7.00
July	3.0	6.93
August	3.1	7.18
Summer	9.2	21.11
Total	×4	×4
Year's		
Total	36.8	$ 84.44

presented in Table 1-1. For June, July, and August, the only gas used was for the water heater (this house has electric appliances), so the annual water-heating gas requirement is $84.44. Table 1-2 shows how this total is developed. Putting these figures into our formula for gas: $(128{,}800 - 36{,}800) \times 1035 = 95{,}220{,}000$ Btu. Looking at economics alone, the owner of the house in this example would not be wise to invest in a solar room heater. Subtracting the hot water portion of the bill, it would take *sixty-eight years*, at present gas prices, to pay for a $6000 system which was "sized" to provide 60% of the home's heating load. Solar heating systems are not designed to handle 100% of the heating needs—it's just too expensive! Supplementary heaters are needed because occasionally the heat being stored by the solar system is used up after a period of cloudy weather. When this happens, the supplementary heater (electric, gas, oil) provides the needed heat until the sun shines again. Although it varies from case to case, a typical solar heater might be designed to provide 50% to 60% of the home's heat with a capability of storing solar heat for two sunless days.

If the home in this example were electrically heated, however, and situated in the New England area where present residential rates may average 4.5¢ per kilowatt-hour (kWh), the economics at this stage would favor further consideration of solar heat. We previously calculated that the home required 95,220,000 Btu to heat it each year. Each kilowatt-hour of electricity provides 3413 Btu; therefore, the total number of kilowatt-hours of fuel consumption in our example for the full-year period is:

$$\frac{95{,}220{,}000}{3413} = 27{,}899$$

At 4.5¢ per kilowatt-hour, this homeowner's heating bill becomes $ 0.045 × 27,899 = $ 1255 per year. Again assuming solar energy can handle 60% of the heating load, it may take only eight years to pay off a $ 6000 system. If electric costs continue to increase, the payoff can occur much sooner.

SOLAR WATER HEATERS

A solar water heater may be in the $800 to $1600 price range. For the previous example, 36,800 cu ft of natural gas was the amount used annually for water heating. This converts to some 38 million Btu. Still assuming a solar unit is sized to supply 60% of the hot water requirements, the payback comparisons for a $1600 system are surprising. As shown in Table 1-3, it may take as long as 31 years for a solar system to be economically justifiable. Or it might be written off in only 5 years!

FUEL COST COMPARISONS

I am sure you have concluded that if you are fortunate enough to have natural gas as a fuel source, its price must increase four or five times before solar energy installations at present prices are worthy of consideration. On the other hand, if you use electric resistance heating, solar energy deserves further consideration. Perhaps you are in this category, either having an existing all-electric home or planning to purchase a new one and learning that roughly half of them use all-electric heat.

Figure 1-1 provides a bleak forecast for future electric rates. From 1964 to 1969, the average homeowner's electric cost per kilowatt-hour actually decreased each year. For the period 1970 through 1973, rate increases averaged just over 3% per year. Electricity was still one of our better bargains and

Table 1-3. Payback Comparisons for $1600 Solar Water-Heating System

Fuel	Unit Cost	Annual Savings	Payback Period
Gas	$2.29/1000 cu ft	$ 51	31 years
Electricity	$0.045/kWh	$301	5 years

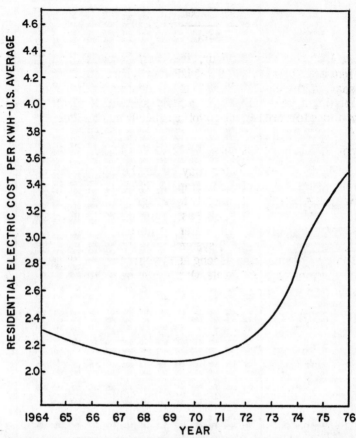

Fig. 1-1. Changes in average residential electric rates over the last 10-year period.

well within the means of the average household. The Arab oil embargo of 1973 put an end to low-cost electricity. 1974 rates rose 18.9% above 1973, and 1975 showed another staggering 13.4% increase. Many analysts predict that residential electric rates will continue to increase, taking another 28% jump by 1980.

The price of natural gas is expected to triple by 1980 if deregulation occurs, and a fuel-oil cost increase of 40% over the same period would not be unrealistic. If you proceed with the economic analysis of a solar unit, I suggest you plan for escalations of this magnitude and calculate your solar payback period accordingly.

Table 1-4. Mean Daily Solar Radiation (Langleys)

States and Stations	JAN.	FEB.	MAR.	APR.	MAY	JUNE	JULY	AUG.	SEPT.	OCT.	NOV.	DEC.	ANNUAL
ALASKA													
Annette	63	115	236	364	437	438	438	341	258	122	59	41	243
Barrow	∉	38	180	380	513	528	429	255	115	41	∉	∉	206
Bethel	38	108	282	444	457	454	376	252	202	115	44	22	233
Fairbanks	16	71	213	376	461	504	434	317	180	82	26	6	224
Mauanuska	32	92	242	356	436	462	409	314	198	100	38	15	224
ARIZONA													
Page	300	382	526	618	695	707	680	596	516	402	310	243	498
Phoenix	301	409	526	638	724	739	658	613	566	449	344	281	520
Tucson	315	391	540	655	729	699	626	588	570	442	356	305	518
ARKANSAS													
Little Rock	188	260	353	446	523	559	556	518	439	343	244	187	385
CALIFORNIA													
Davis	174	257	390	528	625	694	682	612	493	347	222	148	431
Fresno	184	289	427	552	647	702	682	621	510	376	250	161	450
Inyokern (China Lake)	306	412	562	683	772	819	772	729	635	467	363	300	568
LaJolla	244	302	397	457	506	487	497	464	389	320	277	221	380
Los Angeles WBAS	248	331	470	515	572	596	641	581	503	373	289	241	463
Los Angeles WBO	243	327	436	483	555	584	651	581	500	362	281	234	436
Riverside	275	367	478	541	623	680	673	618	535	407	319	270	483
Santa Maria	263	346	482	552	635	694	680	613	524	419	313	252	481
Soda Springs	223	316	374	551	615	691	760	681	510	357	248	182	459
COLORADO													
Boulder	201	268	401	460	460	525	520	439	412	310	222	182	367
Grand Junction	227	324	434	546	615	708	676	595	514	373	260	212	456
Grand Lake (Granby)	212	313	423	512	552	632	600	505	470	361	234	184	417
DISTRICT OF COLUMBIA	174	266	344	411	551	494	536	446	375	299	211	166	356
American University	158	231	322	398	467	510	496	440	364	278	192	141	333
Silver Hill	177	247	342	438	513	555	511	457	391	293	202	156	357
FLORIDA													
Apalachicola	298	367	441	535	603	578	529	511	456	413	332	262	444
Belle Isle	297	330	412	463	483	464	488	461	400	366	313	291	397
Gainsville	267	343	427	517	579	521	488	483	418	347	300	233	410
Miami Airport	349	415	489	540	553	532	532	505	440	384	353	316	451
Tallahassee	274	311	423	499	547	521	508	542	*	*	292	230	—
Tampa	327	391	474	539	596	574	534	494	452	400	356	300	453
GEORGIA													
Atlanta	218	290	380	488	533	562	532	508	416	344	268	211	396
Griffin	234	295	385	522	570	577	556	522	435	368	283	201	413
HAWAII													
Honolulu	363	422	516	559	617	615	615	612	573	507	426	371	516
Mauna Loa Obs.	522	576	680	689	727	*	703	642	602	560	504	481	—
Pearl Harbor	359	400	487	529	573	566	598	567	539	466	386	343	484
IDAHO													
Boise	138	236	342	485	585	636	670	576	460	301	182	124	395
Twin Falls	163	240	355	462	552	592	602	540	432	286	176	131	378
ILLINOIS													
Chicago	96	147	227	331	424	458	473	403	313	207	120	76	273
Lemont	170	242	340	402	506	553	540	498	398	275	165	138	352
INDIANA													
Indianapolis	144	213	316	396	488	543	541	490	405	293	177	132	345
IOWA													
Ames	174	253	326	403	480	541	436	460	367	274	187	143	345
KANSAS													
Dodge City	255	316	418	528	568	650	642	592	493	380	285	234	447
Manhattan	192	264	345	433	527	551	531	526	410	292	227	156	371
KENTUCKY													
Lexington	172	263	357	480	581	628	617	563	494	357	245	174	411
LOUISIANNA													
Lake Charles	245	306	397	481	555	591	526	511	449	402	300	250	418
New Orleans	214	259	335	412	449	443	417	416	383	357	278	198	347
Shreveport	232	292	384	446	558	557	578	528	414	354	254	205	400
MAINE													
Caribou	133	231	364	400	476	470	508	448	336	212	111	107	316
Portland	152	235	352	409	514	539	561	488	383	278	157	137	350
MASSACHUSETTS													
Amherst	116	*	300	*	431	514	*	*	*	*	152	124	—
Blue Hill	153	228	319	389	469	510	502	449	354	266	162	135	328
Boston	129	194	290	350	445	483	486	411	334	235	136	115	301
Cambridge	153	235	323	400	420	476	482	464	367	253	164	124	322
East Wareham	140	218	305	385	452	508	495	436	365	258	163	140	322
Lynn	118	209	300	394	454	549	528	432	341	241	135	107	317
MICHIGAN													
East Lansing	121	210	309	359	483	547	540	466	373	255	136	108	311
Sault Ste. Marie	130	225	356	416	523	557	573	472	322	216	105	96	333
MINNESOTA													
St. Cloud	168	260	368	426	496	535	557	486	366	237	146	124	348
MISSOURI													
Columbia (C.O.)	173	251	340	434	530	574	574	522	453	322	225	158	380
Univ. of Missouri	166	248	324	429	501	560	583	509	417	324	177	146	365
MONTANA													
Glasgow	154	258	385	466	568	605	645	531	410	267	154	116	388
Great Falls	140	232	366	434	528	583	639	532	407	264	154	112	366
Summit	122	162	268	414	462	493	560	510	354	216	102	76	312

Table 1-4 (Continued)

States and Stations	JAN.	FEB.	MAR.	APR.	MAY	JUNE	JULY	AUG.	SEPT.	OCT.	NOV.	DEC.	ANNUAL
NEBRASKA													
Lincoln	188	259	350	416	494	544	568	484	396	296	199	159	363
North Omaha	193	299	365	463	516	546	568	519	410	298	204	170	379
NEVADA													
Ely	236	339	468	563	625	712	647	618	518	394	289	218	469
Las Vegas	277	384	519	621	702	748	675	627	551	429	318	258	509
NEW JERSEY													
Seabrook	157	227	318	403	482	527	509	455	385	278	192	140	339
NEW HAMPSHIRE													
Mt. Washington	117	218	238	*	*	*	*	*	*	*	*	96	---
NEW MEXICO													
Albuquerque	303	386	511	618	686	726	683	626	554	438	334	276	512
NEW YORK													
Ithaca	116	194	272	334	440	501	515	453	346	231	120	96	302
N.Y. Central Park	130	199	290	369	432	470	459	389	331	242	147	115	298
Sayville	160	249	335	415	494	565	543	462	385	289	186	142	352
Schenectady	130	200	273	338	413	448	441	397	299	218	128	104	282
Upton	155	232	339	428	502	573	543	475	391	293	182	146	355
NORTH CAROLINA													
Greensboro	200	276	354	469	531	564	544	485	406	322	243	197	383
Hatteras	238	317	426	569	635	652	625	562	471	358	282	214	443
Raleigh	235	302	*	466	494	564	535	476	379	307	235	199	---
NORTH DAKOTA													
Bismarck	157	250	356	447	550	590	617	516	390	272	161	124	369
OHIO													
Cleveland	125	183	303	286	502	562	562	494	278	289	141	115	335
Columbus	128	200	297	391	471	562	542	477	422	286	176	129	340
Put-in-Bay	126	204	302	386	468	544	561	487	382	275	144	109	332
OKLAHOMA													
Okla. City	251	319	409	494	536	615	610	593	487	377	291	240	436
Stillwater	205	289	390	454	504	600	596	545	455	354	269	209	405
OREGON													
Astoria	90	162	270	375	492	469	539	461	354	209	111	79	301
Corvallis	89	*	287	406	517	570	676	558	397	235	144	80	---
Medford	116	215	336	482	592	652	698	605	447	279	149	93	389
PENNSYLVANIA													
Pittsburgh	94	169	216	317	429	491	497	409	339	207	118	77	280
State College	133	201	295	380	456	518	511	444	358	256	149	118	318
RHODE ISLAND													
Newport	155	232	334	405	477	527	513	455	377	271	176	139	338
SOUTH CAROLINA													
Charleston	252	314	388	512	551	564	520	501	404	338	286	225	404
SOUTH DAKOTA													
Rapid City	183	277	400	482	532	585	590	541	435	315	204	158	392
TENNESSEE													
Nashville	149	228	322	432	503	551	530	473	403	308	208	150	355
Oak Ridge	161	239	331	450	518	551	526	478	416	318	213	163	364
TEXAS													
Brownsville	297	341	402	456	564	610	627	568	475	411	296	263	442
El Paso	333	430	547	654	714	729	666	640	576	460	372	313	536
Ft. Worth	250	320	427	488	562	651	613	593	503	403	306	245	445
Midland	283	358	476	550	611	617	608	574	522	396	325	275	466
San Antonio	279	347	417	445	541	612	639	585	493	398	295	256	442
UTAH													
Flaming Gorge	238	298	443	522	565	650	599	538	425	352	262	215	426
Salt Lake City	163	256	354	479	570	621	620	551	446	316	204	146	394
VIRGINIA													
Mt. Weather	172	274	338	414	508	525	510	430	375	381	202	168	350
WASHINGTON													
North Head	*	167	257	432	509	487	486	436	321	205	122	77	---
Friday Harbor	87	157	274	418	514	578	586	507	351	194	102	75	320
Prosser	117	222	351	521	616	680	707	604	458	274	136	100	399
Pullman	121	205	304	462	558	653	699	562	410	245	146	96	372
Univ. of Wash.	67	126	245	364	445	461	496	435	299	170	93	59	272
Seattle-Tacoma	75	139	265	403	503	511	566	452	324	188	104	64	300
Spokane	119	204	321	474	563	596	665	556	404	225	131	75	361
WISCONSIN													
Madison	148	220	313	394	466	514	531	452	348	241	145	115	324
WYOMING													
Lander	226	324	452	548	587	678	651	586	472	254	239	196	443
Laramie	216	295	424	508	554	643	606	536	438	324	229	186	408
ISLAND STATIONS													
Canton Island	588	626	634	604	561	549	550	597	640	651	600	572	597
San Juan, P.R.	404	481	580	622	519	536	639	549	531	460	411	411	512
Swan Island	442	496	615	646	625	544	588	591	535	457	394	382	526
Wake Island	438	518	577	627	642	656	629	623	587	525	482	421	560

*   insufficient data collected
--- incomplete monthly data
≁   Barrow is in darkness during the winter months

Langley is the unit used to denote one gram calorie per square centimeter.

Climatic Atlas of the United States,
U.S. Department of Commerce

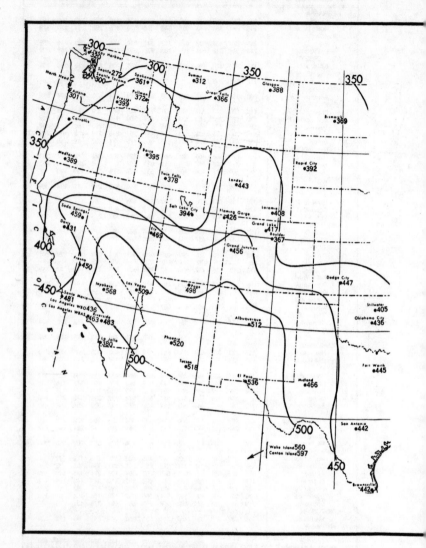

LOCAL WEATHER CONSIDERATIONS

Now that you know your annual heating requirements, is there sufficient sunlight in your area to provide economical fuel for a solar heater? You start to answer this question by referring to historical data for key U.S. cities tabulated in Table 1-4. If you do not find your particular city listed, but there is a local airport near you, chances are the airport's

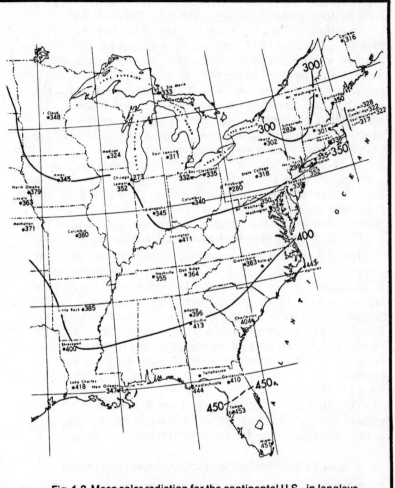

Fig. 1-2. Mean solar radiation for the continental U.S., in langleys.

operations office has the data you need and would be willing to supply it to you. Figure 1-2 is a sketched map of the continental U.S., and offers radiation figures on a locale basis.

Let's take some example cities and use the chart of Table 1-4 to compare their weather during the heating season, which generally extends from October through April. The mean daily solar radiation is given in *langleys*, a measure of the total solar radiation falling on a horizontal surface. One langley per day is equivalent to 3.687 Btu per square foot per day. The langley reading, then, gives a measure of the solar *fuel* available.

In estimating heating needs it is important to have a good idea as to the number of days during a given year that home heating will be required. Research has shown that home heaters will be used when the outdoor temperature drops below 65°F. The further below 65°F the temperature falls, the more heat will be required to make a house comfortable. This relationship gives rise to the term "heating degree days," which is the number of degrees below 65° the daily average temperature reaches during a given season.

In Los Angeles, for example, the average daily temperature is 64.1°F during July. This figure—the average daily temperature—is subtracted from 65°F to give the number of degrees below 65°F on a given day, 0.9°F. Then 0.9°F is multiplied by 31—the number of days in July—to give the total heating degree days for Los Angeles in July: 28.

The degree day then provides a measure of the heat *demand* for a specific period and region. Dividing the radiation R available by the degree-day D requirements over the heating season for a given community provides a useful number, which we'll call a *solar factor F*, for our evaluation: $F = R/D$. For examples, Table 1-5 lists three test cities with langley figures and heating degree days. The *higher* the solar factor in the last column, the more favorable the local weather conditions for solar systems. (Notice that Grand Junction's solar factor is 0.44.)

The other part of the analysis, though, is the *cost* of your present fuel and what your present bill totals for the season. It is self-defeating to pay for an expensive solar room heater if

Table 1-5. Determining Solar Factor, October Through April

CITY	MEAN DAILY SOLAR RADIATION (LANGLEYS), R	HEATING DEOREE DAYS, D	SOLAR FACTOR, F (F=R/D)
Spokane, Washington	1549	6030	0.26
Grand Junction, Colorado	2376	5444	0.44
Boston, Massachusetts	1449	5321	0.27

you live in Miami Beach and do not require heat. On the other hand, a solar water heater which can be used year round is probably a good investment for the Miami resident. Take the home in our earlier example and assume it is located in each of the three test cities. Further assume that electric heat rather than gas is used. In the example, the home used 87,800 cu ft of gas for room heating during the October-to-April season (109,500 less 21,700 used for the water heater). Converting this to an equivalent amount of electricity:

$$87,800 \text{ cu ft} \times 1035 = 90,873,000 \text{ Btu}$$

And:

$$\frac{90,873,000}{3413} = 26,625 \text{ kWh}$$

Once the seasonal heating bill is determined, if you multiply it by the solar factor just calculated, the product gives a meaningful guideline as to the suitability of solar room heating. Table 1-6 shows the calculations for suitability. In this example, the same "load" of 26,625 was used for simplicity even though weather conditions (that is, the total number of degree days for the heating season) varies somewhat between these cities. As a rule of thumb at this stage of the investigation, I would suggest that a suitability index below 300 would merit little consideration for solar room heating. The residence in Spokane has a low electric rate and minimum sunshine—solar power is not practical. Boston's electric rate is so high it offsets marginal sunshine, and solar power should be considered. Grand Junction has considerable sunshine, and if escalating electric rates are expected, a solar installation could be a good buy.

Figure 1-3 is a generalized U. S. map that shows annual normal heating degree days by locale. The scale is so

Table 1-6. Determining Solar Heat Suitability

CITY	HEAT POWER REQD, kWh	RATE ¢/kWh	OCTOBER-APRIL HEATING COST C	SOLAR FACTOR R/D	SUITABILITY INDEX C×R/D
Spokane, Washington	26,625	1.48	$ 394	0.26	102
Grand Junction, Colorado	26,625	3.36	$ 895	0.44	394
Boston, Massachusetts	26,625	5.59	$1488	0.27	402

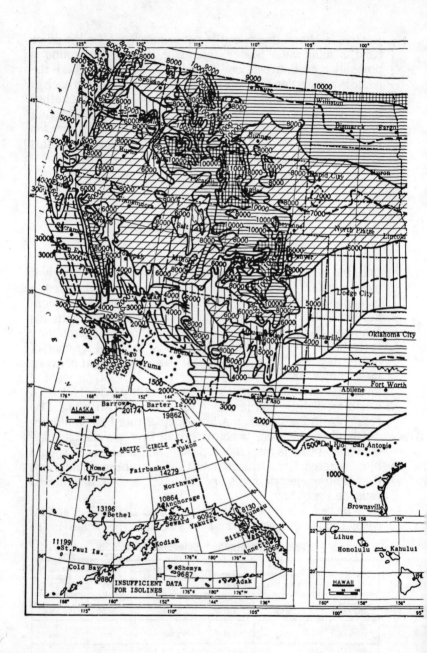

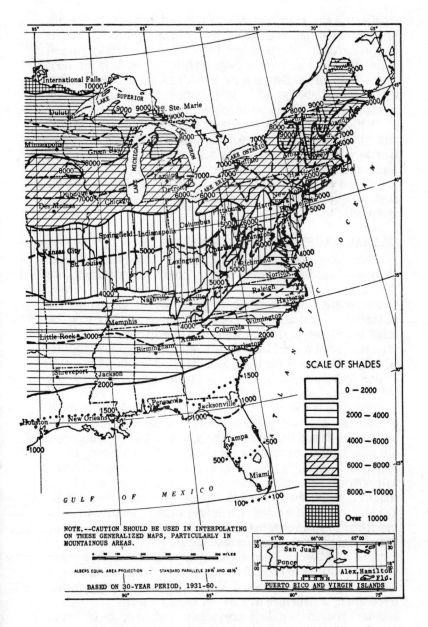

Fig. 1-3. Annual heating degree days for the U.S.

small—and the map requires so much detail—that it is not
fully readable; but you should get a fair idea of the annual *D*
for your area by interpolation. Table 1-7, presented at the end
of this chapter, lists normal total heating degree days for most
major U. S. cities. Between the two—the map and the chart—
there should be enough information for you to draw
meaningful conclusions as to degree days for your area.

You should compute the seasonal heating bill, solar factor,
and suitability index for your individual residence and city.
Compare your findings with my analysis on the test cities and
make an intermediate decision on solar heating. If you decide
to proceed with the investigation, the following factors are the
next to be considered: distribution system, solar exposure,
and insulation.

CHARACTERISTICS OF THE HOME

Most readers of this book are investigating the use of solar
energy to heat their present houses, not to incorporate it into
the design of new ones. This requires that many
characteristics of the home be explored to determine its
suitability. You must have a distribution system to carry the
solar heat from a storage tank into the living area. If you
presently have a good forced-air heating system, it should be
adequate to convert for solar use. On the other hand, electric
heated floor or ceiling panels or hot water baseboard systems
will not do the job.

Sunshine is the fuel for the solar furnace, and there must
be adequate provision made to insure that the solar collector is
not shaded at any time during the day. For heating purposes,
the solar collectors operate best when they are facing south
and tilted to an angle equivalent to your latitude plus $10°$. They
will operate with other orientation, but at lower efficiency,
requiring more square footage of panel at a much higher cost.
The sun travels at a low angle during winter months, and it is
important to avoid shading by any adjacent buildings, trees, or
the natural topography of the land.

The question of "sun rights," or whether solar system
users are entitled to an unobstructed view of the sun, is a legal
matter that must be resolved. Certainly a neighbor's growing
tree, or a new structure which later blocks the effectiveness of
a solar system you had previously installed, is of great
concern. Also, if you live in an area that experiences frequent
and dense fog, this could present a problem.

Solar collectors are generally mounted on flat or pitched roofs or on ground frames, as shown in Fig. 1-4. The roof is the most popular spot because this is the space that is normally most usable, and the collectors can help to insulate the roof, thus reducing heating and air-conditioning loads.

Although more precise methods of determining collector size will be covered in Chapter 5, you should plan an area for collector mounting equivalent to one-half the square footage of the heated area of your house. That is, if you heat 2000 sq ft, 1000 sq ft of roof or ground area with an unshaded southern

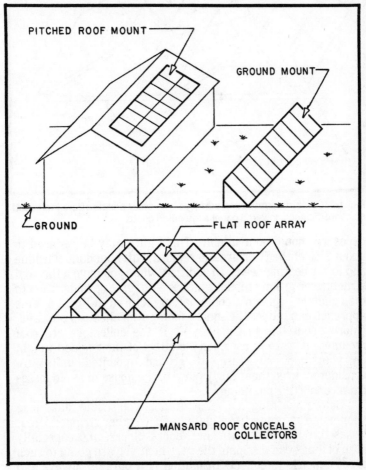

Fig. 1-4. Typical locations for mounting solar collectors.

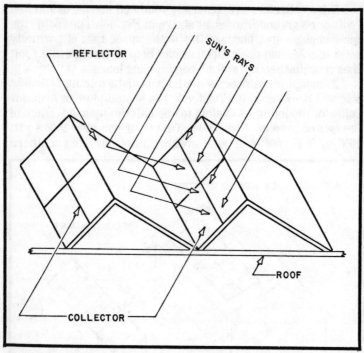

Fig. 1-5. Combining reflecting surfaces with solar panels offers increased system efficiency, lowered panel acquisition costs.

exposure should be available. This figure may be reduced to about 33% of the floor area in regions with abundant sunshine and lower heating needs. In addition, when you have a flat roof structure or ground mount to work with, give consideration to the collector—reflector combination pictured in Fig. 1-5. This approach can reduce the square footage of collectors required. (More about this in Chapter 3.) If the collectors are roof mounted, be sure to consider the effect of their added weight on your roof structure. If ground mounted units are considered, keep them fairly close to the house to avoid losses from connecting plumbing.

Before investing in a solar furnace, you should make sure your home is properly insulated and weather-stripped. Heat losses through walls, windows, doors, floors, and especially attic ceilings can dissipate the very heat you are going to such great expense to collect. Insulation is a bargain always and should be your first consideration.

GOVERNMENT INCENTIVES

Earlier in this chapter some examples were given of the time required to pay off a solar system in fuel savings alone. Although system costs will come down with volume production and further technology, both federal and state governments have recognized the need to help the homeowner financially. The government is motivated by the fact that approximately 25% of all energy used in this country is for the heating and cooling of buildings (including hot water applications).

If the United States is sincere about becoming an energy-independent nation, alternative sources such as solar energy must be encouraged. Legislators, therefore, have been busy proposing laws to provide tax incentives for solar installations. Some states have already passed laws that would help you afford the extra cost of a solar heating system, among them Colorado, Maryland, Montana, New Hampshire, North Dakota, South Dakota, and Texas. Arizona taxpayers can amortize the system cost over five years by deducting it when computing state income tax. Indiana property owners may exempt up to $2000 of the cost of a solar heating system installed in a commercial or residential building from its assessed valuation. Other states considering similar legislation are California, Connecticut, Illinois, Massachusetts, Michigan, Minnesota, New Jersey, New Mexico, New York, Oregon, Pennsylvania, South Carolina, Virginia, and Wisconsin.

Considerable federal legislation designed to benefit solar users was introduced in the 94th Congress. Bills HR-3849, HR-5460, and S-2163 seek to establish a low-interest loan program to assist homeowners and builders in purchasing and installing solar heating equipment.

Several other bills were introduced permitting an income tax reduction with respect to the purchase and installation of solar heating and cooling equipment. These include S-28, S-168, S-1379, HR-1697, and HR-5005. Your congressman can give you the current status of these and other bills relating to solar energy which may influence your decision to buy. It is apparent from the legislators' activities that both federal and state lawmakers recognize the need to help the homeowner pay the added cost of a solar heating system.

SUMMARY

To summarize and review this chapter, the following questions should be answered for your specific case:

(1) Is your annual heating bill over $500?
(2) Is your suitability index 300 or over?
(3) Do you presently have a forced-air furnace?
(4) Do you have an adequate unshaded area for mounting collectors?
(5) Is your home insulated and weather-stripped?
(6) Do you believe that the cost of your present heating fuel will continue to increase?
(7) Do you have a basement or location near the house where a heat storage tank could be buried?

If the answer to all these questions is yes, I would encourage you to seriously consider a solar room heating system from an economic standpoint. If your interest is in a solar water or swimming pool heater, a similar analysis should be made, using the information provided in Chapters 6 and 7.

Table 1-7. Normal Total Heating Degree Days, Monthly and Annual (Base 56°)

STATE AND STATION	JULY	AUG.	SEPT.	OCT.	NOV.	DEC.	JAN.	FEB.	MAR.	APR.	MAY	JUNE	ANNUAL
ALABAMA													
Birmingham	0	0	6	93	363	555	592	462	363	108	9	0	2551
Huntsville	0	0	12	127	426	663	694	557	434	138	19	0	3070
Mobile	0	0	0	22	213	357	415	300	211	42	0	0	1560
Montgomery	0	0	0	68	330	527	543	417	316	90	0	0	2291
ALASKA													
Anchorage	245	291	516	930	1284	1572	1631	1316	1293	879	592	315	10864
Annette	242	208	327	567	738	899	949	837	843	648	490	321	7069
Barrow	803	840	1035	1500	1971	2362	2517	2332	2468	1944	1445	957	20174
Barter Is.	735	775	987	1482	1944	2337	2536	2369	2477	1923	1373	924	19862
Bethel	319	394	612	1042	1434	1866	1903	1590	1655	1173	806	402	13196
Cold Bay	474	425	525	772	918	1122	1153	1036	1122	951	791	591	9880
Cordova	366	391	522	781	1017	1221	1299	1086	1113	864	660	444	9764
Fairbanks	171	332	642	1203	1833	2254	2359	1901	1739	1068	555	222	14279
Juneau	301	338	483	725	921	1135	1237	1070	1073	810	601	381	9075
King Salmon	313	322	513	908	1290	1606	1600	1333	1411	966	673	408	11343
Kotzebue	381	446	723	1249	1728	2127	2192	1932	2080	1554	1057	636	16105
McGrath	208	338	633	1184	1791	2232	2294	1817	1758	1122	648	258	14283
Nome	481	496	693	1094	1455	1820	1879	1666	1770	1314	930	573	14171
Saint Paul	605	539	612	862	963	1197	1228	1168	1265	1098	936	726	11199
Shemya	577	475	501	784	876	1042	1045	958	1011	885	837	696	9687
Yakutat	338	347	474	716	936	1144	1169	1019	1042	840	632	435	9092
ARIZONA													
Flagstaff	46	68	201	558	867	1073	1169	991	991	651	437	180	7152
Phoenix	0	0	0	22	234	415	474	328	217	75	0	0	1765
Prescott	0	0	27	245	579	797	865	711	605	360	158	15	4362
Tucson	0	0	0	25	231	406	471	344	242	75	6	0	1800
Winslow	0	0	6	245	711	1008	1054	770	601	291	96	0	4782
Yuma	0	0	0	0	148	319	363	228	130	29	0	0	1217
ARKANSAS													
Fort Smith	0	0	12	127	450	704	781	596	456	144	22	0	3292
Little Rock	0	0	9	127	465	716	756	577	434	126	9	0	3219
Texarkana	0	0	0	78	345	561	626	468	350	105	0	0	2533
CALIFORNIA													
Bakersfield	0	0	0	37	282	502	546	364	267	105	19	0	2122
Bishop	0	0	42	248	576	797	874	666	539	306	143	36	4227
Blue Canyon	34	50	120	347	579	766	865	781	791	582	397	195	5507
Burbank	0	0	6	43	177	301	366	277	239	138	81	18	1646
Eureka	270	257	258	329	414	499	546	470	505	438	372	285	4643
Fresno	0	0	0	78	339	558	586	406	319	150	56	0	2492
Long Beach	0	0	12	40	156	288	375	297	267	168	90	18	1711
Los Angeles	28	22	42	78	180	291	372	302	288	219	158	81	2061

Table 1-7. (Continued)

STATE AND STATION	JULY	AUG.	SEPT.	OCT.	NOV.	DEC.	JAN.	FEB.	MAR.	APR.	MAY	JUNE	ANNUAL
Mt. Shasta	25	34	123	406	696	902	983	784	738	525	347	159	5722
Oakland	53	50	45	127	309	481	527	400	353	255	180	90	2870
Point Arguello	202	186	162	205	291	400	474	392	403	339	298	243	3595
Red Bluff	0	0	0	53	318	555	605	428	341	168	47	0	2515
Sacramento	0	0	12	81	363	577	614	442	360	216	102	6	2773
Sandberg	0	0	30	202	480	691	778	661	620	426	264	57	4209
San Diego	6	0	15	37	123	251	313	249	202	123	84	36	1439
San Francisco	81	78	60	143	306	462	508	395	363	279	214	126	3015
Santa Catalina	16	0	9	50	165	279	353	308	326	249	192	105	2052
Santa Maria	99	93	96	146	270	391	459	370	363	282	233	165	2967
COLORADO													
Alamosa	65	99	279	639	1065	1420	1476	1162	1020	696	440	168	8529
Colo. Springs	9	25	132	456	825	1032	1128	938	893	582	319	84	6423
Denver	6	9	117	428	819	1035	1132	938	887	558	288	66	6283
Grand Junction	0	0	30	313	786	1113	1209	907	729	387	146	21	5641
Pueblo	0	0	54	326	750	986	1085	871	772	429	174	15	5462
CONNECTICUT													
Bridgeport	0	0	66	307	615	986	1079	966	853	510	208	27	5617
Hartford	0	6	99	372	711	1119	1209	1061	899	495	177	24	6172
New Haven	0	12	87	347	648	1011	1097	991	871	543	245	45	5897
DELAWARE													
Wilmington	0	0	51	270	588	927	980	874	735	387	112	6	4930
FLORIDA													
Apalachicola	0	0	0	16	153	319	347	260	180	33	0	0	1308
Daytona Beach	0	0	0	0	75	211	248	190	140	15	0	0	879
Fort Myers	0	0	0	0	24	109	146	101	62	0	0	0	442
Jacksonville	0	0	0	12	144	310	332	246	174	21	0	0	1239
Key West	0	0	0	0	0	28	40	31	9	0	0	0	108
Lakeland	0	0	0	0	57	164	195	146	99	0	0	0	661
Miami Beach	0	0	0	0	0	40	56	36	9	0	0	0	141
Orlando	0	0	0	0	72	198	220	165	105	6	0	0	766
Pensacola	0	0	0	19	195	353	400	277	183	36	0	0	1463
Tallahassee	0	0	0	28	198	360	375	286	202	36	0	0	1485
Tampa	0	0	0	0	60	171	202	148	102	0	0	0	683
West Palm Beach	0	0	0	0	6	65	87	64	31	0	0	0	253
GEORGIA													
Athens	0	0	12	115	405	632	642	529	431	141	22	0	2929
Atlanta	0	0	18	127	414	626	639	529	437	168	25	0	2983
Augusta	0	0	0	78	333	552	549	445	350	90	0	0	2397
Columbus	0	0	0	87	333	543	552	434	338	96	0	0	2383
Macon	0	0	0	71	297	502	505	403	295	63	0	0	2136
Rome	0	0	24	161	474	701	710	577	468	177	34	0	3326
Savannah	0	0	0	47	246	437	437	353	254	45	0	0	1819
Thomasville	0	0	0	25	198	366	394	305	208	33	0	0	1529
IDAHO													
Boise	0	0	132	415	792	1017	1113	854	722	438	245	81	5809
Idaho Falls 46W	16	34	270	623	1056	1370	1538	1249	1085	651	391	192	8475
Idaho Falls 42 NW	16	40	282	648	1107	1432	1600	1291	1107	657	388	192	8760
Lewiston	0	0	123	403	756	933	1063	815	694	426	239	90	5542
Pocatello	0	0	172	493	900	1166	1324	1058	905	555	319	141	7033
ILLINOIS													
Cairo	0	0	36	164	513	791	856	680	539	195	47	0	3821
Chicago	0	0	81	326	753	1113	1209	1044	890	480	211	48	6155
Moline	0	9	99	335	774	1181	1314	1100	918	450	189	39	6408
Peoria	0	6	87	326	759	1113	1218	1025	849	426	183	33	6025
Rockford	6	9	114	400	837	1221	1333	1137	961	516	236	60	6830
Springfield	0	0	72	291	696	1023	1135	935	769	354	136	18	5429
INDIANA													
Evansville	0	0	66	220	606	896	955	767	620	237	68	0	4435
Fort Wayne	0	9	105	378	783	1135	1178	1028	890	471	189	39	6205
Indianapolis	0	0	90	316	723	1051	1113	949	809	432	177	39	5699
South Bend	0	6	111	372	777	1125	1221	1070	933	525	239	60	6439
IOWA													
Burlington	0	0	93	322	768	1135	1259	1042	859	426	177	33	6114
Des Moines	0	9	99	363	837	1231	1398	1165	967	489	211	39	6808
Dubuque	12	31	156	450	906	1287	1402	1204	1026	546	260	78	7376
Sioux City	0	9	108	369	867	1240	1435	1198	989	483	214	39	6951
Waterloo	12	19	138	428	909	1296	1460	1221	1023	531	229	54	7320
KANSAS													
Concordia	0	0	57	276	705	1023	1163	935	781	372	149	18	5479
Dodge City	0	0	33	251	666	939	1051	840	719	354	124	9	4986
Goodland	0	6	81	381	810	1073	1166	955	884	507	236	42	6141
Topeka	0	0	57	270	672	980	1122	893	722	330	124	12	5182
Wichita	0	0	33	229	618	905	1023	804	645	270	87	6	4620
KENTUCKY													
Covington	0	0	75	291	669	983	1035	893	756	390	149	24	5265
Lexington	0	0	54	239	609	902	946	818	685	325	015	0	4683
Louisville	0	0	54	248	609	890	930	818	682	315	015	9	4660
LOUISIANNA													
Alexandria	0	0	0	56	273	431	471	361	260	69	0	0	1921
Baton Rouge	0	0	0	31	216	369	409	294	208	33	0	0	1560
Burrwood	0	0	0	0	96	214	298	218	171	27	0	0	1024

Table 1-7. (Continued)

STATE AND STATION	JULY	AUG.	SEPT.	OCT.	NOV.	DEC.	JAN.	FEB.	MAR.	APR.	MAY	JUNE	ANNUAL
Lake Charles	0	0	0	19	210	341	381	274	195	39	0	0	1459
New Orleans	0	0	0	19	192	322	363	258	192	39	0	0	1385
Shreveport	0	0	0	47	297	477	552	426	304	81	0	0	2184
MAINE													
Caribou	78	115	336	682	1044	1535	1690	1470	1308	858	468	183	9767
Portland	12	53	195	508	807	1215	1339	1182	1042	675	372	111	7511
MARYLAND													
Baltimore	0	0	48	264	585	905	936	820	679	327	90	0	4654
Frederick	0	0	66	307	624	955	995	876	741	384	127	12	5087
MASSACHUSETTS													
Blue Hill Obs.	0	22	108	381	690	1085	1178	1053	936	579	267	69	6368
Boston	0	9	60	316	603	983	1088	972	846	513	208	36	5634
Nantucket	12	22	93	332	573	896	992	941	896	621	384	129	5891
Pittsfield	25	59	219	524	831	1231	1339	1196	1063	660	326	105	7578
Worcester	6	34	147	450	774	1172	1271	1123	998	612	304	78	6969
MICHIGAN													
Alpena	68	105	273	580	912	1268	1404	1299	1218	777	446	156	8506
Detroit (city)	0	0	87	360	738	1088	1181	1058	936	522	220	42	6232
Escanaba	59	87	243	539	924	1293	1445	1296	1203	777	456	159	8481
Flint	16	40	159	465	843	1212	1330	1198	1066	639	319	90	7377
Grand Rapids	9	28	135	434	804	1147	1259	1134	1011	579	279	75	6894
Lansing	6	22	138	431	813	1163	1262	1142	1011	579	273	69	6909
Marquette	59	81	240	527	936	1268	1411	1268	1187	771	468	177	8393
Muskegon	12	28	120	400	762	1088	1209	1100	995	594	310	78	6696
Sault Ste. Marie	96	105	279	580	951	1367	1525	1380	1277	810	477	201	9048
MINNESOTA													
Duluth	71	109	330	632	1131	1581	1745	1518	1355	840	490	198	10000
Internat'l Falls	71	112	363	701	1236	1724	1919	1621	1414	828	443	174	10606
Minneapolis	22	31	189	505	1014	1454	1631	1380	1166	621	288	81	8382
Rochester	25	34	186	474	1005	1438	1593	1366	1150	630	301	93	8295
Saint Cloud	28	47	225	549	1065	1500	1702	1445	1221	666	326	105	8879
MISSISSIPPI													
Jackson	0	0	0	65	315	502	546	414	310	87	0	0	2239
Meridian	0	0	0	81	339	518	543	417	310	81	0	0	2289
Vicksburg	0	0	0	53	279	462	512	384	282	69	0	0	2041
MISSOURI													
Columbia	0	0	54	251	651	967	1076	874	716	324	121	12	5046
Kansas	0	0	39	220	612	905	1032	818	682	294	109	0	4711
St. Joseph	0	6	60	285	708	1039	1172	949	769	348	133	15	5484
St. Louis	0	0	60	251	627	936	1026	848	704	312	121	15	4900
Springfield	0	0	45	223	600	877	973	781	660	291	105	6	4561
MONTANA													
Billings	6	15	186	487	897	1135	1296	1100	970	570	285	102	7049
Glasgow	31	47	270	608	1104	1466	1711	1439	1187	648	335	150	8996
Great Falls	28	53	258	543	921	1169	1349	1154	1063	642	384	186	7750
Havre	28	53	306	595	1065	1367	1584	1364	1181	657	338	162	8700
Helena	31	59	294	601	1002	1265	1438	1170	1042	651	381	195	8129
Kalispell	50	99	321	654	1020	1240	1401	1134	1029	639	397	207	8191
Miles City	6	6	174	502	972	1296	1504	1252	1057	579	276	99	7723
Missoula	34	74	303	651	1035	1287	1420	1120	970	621	391	219	8125
NEBRASKA													
Grand Island	0	6	108	381	834	1172	1314	1089	908	462	211	45	6530
Lincoln	0	6	75	301	726	1066	1237	1016	834	402	171	30	5864
Norfolk	9	0	111	397	873	1234	1414	1179	983	498	233	48	6979
North Platte	0	6	123	440	885	1166	1271	1039	930	519	248	57	6684
Omaha	0	12	105	357	828	1175	1355	1126	939	465	208	42	6612
Scottsbluff	0	0	138	459	876	1128	1231	1008	921	552	285	75	6673
Valentine	9	12	165	493	942	1237	1395	1176	1045	579	288	84	7425
NEVADA													
Elko	9	34	225	561	924	1197	1314	1036	911	621	409	192	7433
Ely	28	43	234	592	939	1184	1308	1075	977	672	456	225	7733
Las Vegas	0	0	0	78	387	617	688	487	335	111	6	0	2709
Reno	43	87	204	490	801	1026	1073	823	729	510	357	189	6332
Winnemucca	0	34	210	536	876	1091	1172	916	837	573	363	153	6761
HEW HAMPSHIRE													
Concord	6	50	177	505	822	1240	1358	1184	1032	636	298	75	7383
Mt. Wash. Obs.	493	536	720	1057	1341	1742	1820	1663	1652	1260	930	603	12817
NEW JERSEY													
Atlantic City	0	0	39	251	549	880	936	848	741	420	133	15	4812
Newark	0	0	30	248	573	921	983	876	729	381	118	0	4859
Trenton	0	0	57	264	576	924	989	885	753	399	121	12	4980
NEW MEXICO													
Albuquerque	0	0	12	229	642	868	930	703	595	288	81	0	4348
Clayton	0	6	66	310	699	899	986	812	747	429	183	21	5158
Raton	9	28	126	431	825	1048	1116	904	834	543	301	63	6228
Roswell	0	0	18	202	573	806	641	481	201	31	0	37	3793
Silver City	0	0	6	183	525	729	791	605	518	261	87	0	3705
NEW YORK													
Albany	0	19	138	440	777	1194	1311	1156	992	564	239	45	6875
Binghamton (AP)	22	65	201	471	810	1184	1277	1154	1045	645	313	99	7286
Binghamton (PO)	0	28	141	406	732	1107	1190	1081	949	543	229	45	6451

Table 1-7. (Continued)

STATE AND STATION	JULY	AUG.	SEPT.	OCT.	NOV.	DEC.	JAN.	FEB.	MAR.	APR.	MAY	JUNE	ANNUAL
Buffalo	19	37	141	440	777	1156	1256	1145	1039	645	329	78	7062
Central Park	0	0	30	233	540	902	986	885	760	408	118	9	4871
JFK International	0	0	36	248	564	933	1029	935	815	480	167	12	5219
La Guardia	0	0	27	223	528	887	973	879	750	414	124	6	4811
Rochester	9	31	126	415	747	1125	1234	1123	1014	597	279	48	6748
Schenectady	0	22	123	422	756	1159	1283	1131	970	543	211	30	6650
Syracuse	6	28	132	415	744	1153	1271	1140	1004	570	248	45	6756
NORTH CAROLINA													
Asheville	0	0	48	245	555	775	784	683	592	273	87	0	4042
Cape Hatteras	0	0	0	78	273	521	580	518	440	177	25	0	2612
Charlotte	0	0	6	124	438	691	691	582	481	156	22	0	3191
Greensboro	0	0	33	192	513	778	784	672	552	234	47	0	3805
Raleigh	0	0	21	164	450	716	725	616	487	180	34	0	3393
Wilmington	0	0	0	74	291	521	546	462	357	96	0	0	2347
Winston Salem	0	0	21	171	483	747	753	652	524	207	37	0	3595
NORTH DAKOTA													
Bismarck	34	28	222	577	1083	1463	1708	1442	1203	645	329	117	8851
Devils Lake	40	53	273	642	1191	1634	1872	1579	1345	753	381	138	9901
Fargo	28	37	219	574	1107	1569	1789	1520	1262	690	332	99	9226
Williston	31	43	261	601	1122	1513	1758	1473	1262	681	357	141	9243
OHIO													
Akron	0	9	96	381	726	1070	1138	1016	871	489	202	39	6037
Cincinnati	0	0	54	248	612	921	970	837	701	336	118	9	4806
Cleveland	9	25	105	384	738	1088	1159	1047	918	552	260	66	6351
Columbus	0	6	84	347	714	1039	1088	949	809	426	171	27	5660
Dayton	0	6	78	310	696	1045	1097	955	809	429	167	30	5622
Mansfield	9	22	114	397	768	1110	1169	1042	924	543	245	60	6403
Sandusky	0	6	6	313	684	1032	1107	991	868	495	198	36	5796
Toledo	0	16	117	406	792	1138	1200	1056	921	543	242	60	6494
Youngstown	0	19	120	412	771	1104	1169	1047	921	540	248	60	6417
OKLAHOMA													
Okla. City	0	0	15	164	498	766	868	664	527	189	34	0	3725
Tulsa	0	0	18	158	522	787	893	683	539	213	47	0	3860
OREGON													
Astoria	146	130	210	375	561	679	753	622	636	480	363	231	5186
Burns	12	37	210	515	867	1113	1246	988	856	570	366	177	6957
Eugene	34	34	129	366	585	719	803	627	589	426	279	135	4726
Meacham	84	124	288	580	918	1091	1209	1005	983	726	527	339	7874
Medford	0	0	78	372	678	871	918	697	642	432	242	78	5008
Pendleton	0	0	111	350	711	884	1017	773	617	396	205	63	5127
Portland	25	28	114	335	597	735	825	644	586	396	245	105	4635
Roseburg	22	16	105	329	567	713	766	608	570	405	267	123	4491
Salem	37	31	111	338	594	729	822	647	611	417	273	144	4754
Sexton Summit	81	81	171	443	666	874	958	809	818	609	465	279	6254
PENNSYLVANIA													
Allentown	0	0	90	353	693	1045	1116	1002	849	471	167	24	5810
Erie	0	25	102	391	714	1063	1169	1081	973	585	288	60	6451
Harrisburg	0	0	63	298	648	992	1045	907	766	396	124	12	5251
Philadelphia	0	0	60	291	621	964	1014	890	744	390	115	12	5101
Pittsburgh	0	9	105	375	726	1063	1119	1002	874	480	195	39	5987
Reading	0	0	54	257	597	939	1001	885	735	372	105	0	4945
Scranton	0	19	132	434	762	1104	1156	1028	893	498	195	33	6254
Williamsport	0	9	111	375	717	1073	1122	1002	856	468	177	24	5934
RHODE ISLAND													
Block Is.	0	16	78	307	594	902	1020	955	877	612	344	99	5804
Providence	0	16	96	372	660	1023	1110	988	868	534	236	51	5954
SOUTH CAROLINA													
Charleston	0	0	0	59	282	471	487	389	291	54	0	0	2033
Columbia	0	0	0	84	345	577	570	470	357	81	0	0	2484
Florence	0	0	0	78	315	552	552	459	347	84	0	0	2387
Greenville	0	0	0	112	387	636	648	535	434	120	12	0	2884
Spartanburg	0	0	15	130	417	667	663	560	453	144	25	0	3074
SOUTH DAKOTA													
Huron	9	12	165	508	1014	1432	1628	1355	1125	600	288	87	8223
Rapid City	22	12	165	481	897	1172	1333	1145	1051	615	326	126	7345
Sioux Falls	19	25	168	462	972	1361	1544	1285	1082	573	270	78	7839
TENNESSEE													
Bristol	0	0	51	236	573	828	828	700	598	261	68	0	4143
Chattanooga	0	0	18	143	468	698	722	577	453	150	25	0	3254
Knoxville	0	0	30	171	489	725	732	613	493	198	43	0	3494
Memphis	0	0	18	130	447	698	729	585	456	147	22	0	3232
Nashville	0	0	30	158	495	732	778	644	512	189	40	0	3578
Oak Ridge (CO)	0	0	39	192	531	772	778	669	552	228	56	0	3817
TEXAS													
Abilene	0	0	0	99	366	586	642	470	347	114	0	0	2624
Amarillo	0	0	18	205	570	797	877	664	546	252	56	0	3985
Austin	0	0	0	31	225	388	468	325	223	51	0	0	1711
Brownsville	0	0	0	0	66	149	205	106	74	0	0	0	600
Corpus Christi	0	0	0	0	120	220	291	174	109	0	0	0	914
Dallas	0	0	0	62	321	524	601	440	319	90	6	0	2363
El Paso	0	0	0	84	414	648	685	445	319	105	0	0	2700
Forth Worth	0	0	0	65	324	536	614	448	319	99	0	0	2405
Galveston	0	0	0	0	138	270	350	258	189	30	0	0	1235

Table 1-7. (Continued)

STATE AND STATION	JULY	AUG.	SEPT.	OCT.	NOV.	DEC.	JAN.	FEB.	MAR.	APR.	MAY	JUNE	ANNUAL
Laredo	0	0	0	0	105	217	267	134	74	0	0	0	797
Lubbock	0	0	18	174	513	744	800	613	484	201	31	0	3578
Midland	0	0	0	87	381	592	651	468	322	90	0	0	2591
Port Arthur	0	0	0	22	207	329	384	274	192	39	0	0	1447
San Angelo	0	0	0	68	318	536	567	412	288	66	0	0	2255
San Antonio	0	0	0	31	207	363	428	286	195	39	0	0	1549
Victoria	0	0	0	6	150	270	344	230	152	21	0	0	1173
Waco	0	0	0	43	270	456	536	389	270	66	0	0	2030
Wichita Falls	0	0	0	99	381	632	698	518	378	120	6	0	2832
UTAH													
Milford	0	0	99	443	867	1141	1252	988	822	519	279	87	6497
Salt Lake City	0	0	81	419	849	1082	1172	910	763	459	233	84	6052
Wendover	0	0	48	372	822	1091	1178	902	729	408	177	51	5778
VERMONT													
Burlington	28	65	207	539	891	1349	1513	1333	1187	714	353	90	8269
VIRGINIA													
Cape Henry	0	0	0	112	360	645	694	633	536	246	53	0	3279
Lynchburg	0	0	51	223	540	822	849	731	605	267	78	0	4166
Norfolk	0	0	0	136	408	698	738	655	533	216	37	0	3421
Richmond	0	0	36	214	495	784	815	703	546	219	53	0	3865
Roanoke	0	0	51	229	549	825	834	722	614	261	65	0	4150
Wash. Nat'l AP	0	0	33	217	519	834	871	762	626	288	74	0	4224
WASHINGTON													
Olympia	68	71	198	422	636	753	834	675	645	450	307	177	5236
Seattle	50	47	129	329	543	657	738	599	577	396	242	117	4424
Seattle Boeing	34	40	147	384	624	763	831	655	608	411	242	99	4838
Seattle Tacoma	56	62	162	391	633	750	828	678	657	474	295	159	5145
Spokane	9	25	168	493	879	1082	1231	980	834	531	288	135	6655
Stampede Pass	273	291	393	701	1008	1178	1287	1075	1085	855	654	483	9283
Tatoosh Is.	295	279	306	406	534	639	713	613	645	525	431	333	5719
Walla Walla	0	0	87	310	681	834	986	745	589	342	177	45	4805
Yakima	0	12	144	450	828	1039	1163	868	713	435	220	69	5941
WEST VIRGINIA													
Charleston	0	0	63	254	591	865	880	770	648	300	96	9	4476
Elkins	9	25	135	400	729	992	1008	896	791	444	198	48	5675
Huntington	0	0	63	257	585	856	880	764	636	294	99	12	4446
Parkersburg	0	0	60	264	606	905	942	826	691	339	115	6	4754
WISCONSIN													
Green Bay	28	50	174	484	924	1333	1494	1313	1141	654	335	99	8029
LaCrosse	12	19	153	437	924	1339	1504	1277	1070	540	245	69	7589
Madison	25	40	174	474	930	1330	1473	1274	1113	618	310	102	7863
Milwaukee	43	47	174	471	876	1252	1376	1193	1054	642	372	135	7635
WYOMING													
Casper	6	16	192	524	942	1169	1290	1084	1020	657	381	129	7410
Cheyenne	19	31	210	543	924	1101	1228	1056	1011	672	381	102	7278
Lander	6	19	204	555	1020	1299	1417	1145	1017	654	381	153	7870
Sheridan	25	31	219	539	948	1200	1355	1154	1054	642	366	150	7683

Climatic Atlas of the United States, U.S. Department of Commerce

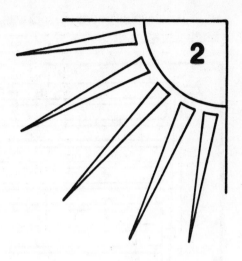

2

How Does It Work?

There are four main parts to a solar heating system: the collector, the heat storage tank, a control system, and an auxiliary energy source. The sun heats the collector, which is normally covered by glass or other transparent material; the collector traps heat in a method similar to an automobile in the sunshine with the windows rolled up. This heat is transferred to a working fluid, such as water or water plus an antifreeze mixture, circulating through the collector. The heated fluid is pumped, either directly or through a heat exchanger, into an insulated storage tank. Storage of the heat is necessary because the sun shines only by day, and many days are cloudy. Yet, heating demands continue on overcast days, in the evening, and before sunrise. When the water in the storage tank is sufficiently hot, it can be used in the following ways:

- To supply hot water.
- As a heat source for a forced-air furnace.
- To operate a heat-driven cooling system.

Auxiliary energy is used to supplement the solar system whenever the heat being stored is used up after a period of cloudy weather. When this happens, the auxiliary heating system (using gas, electricity, or fuel oil) provides the needed heat until the sun shines again.

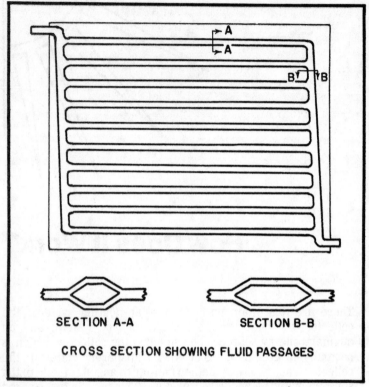

Fig. 2-1. Construction details of a metal absorber plate with integral fluid passages.

A BASIC SYSTEM

The collector can be as simple as a flat metal plate insulated on its underside and painted black to absorb the heat of the sun. It might have passages through which the working fluid passes to be heated. Let's develop the construction of a *flat plate* or basic type of solar collector from its component parts.

Figure 2-1 shows a metal plate with built-in passages—the type most commonly used today. Typically, these metal plates, called *absorbers* or *collector plates*, are made of aluminum or copper, as these metals are good conductors of heat. On a sunny day, fluid flowing through an absorber of this type would pick up some heat from the sun, but not an amount sufficient enough to operate the system. Much of the energy striking the plate would be reflected. In addition, any breeze would cool the plate and the fluid flowing through it.

Insulation of the absorber minimizes heat losses. Figure 2-2 shows the absorber in a frame with insulation on the back side and covered with one pane of glass. When the unit is properly sealed, the glass traps solar radiation, which heats the insulated absorber plates. This heat is transferred to the fluid flowing through the absorber passages or tubes.

To illustrate this cycle, Fig. 2-3 shows roof mounted solar collectors connected to a *heat exchanger*. A heat exchanger is constructed using several coils of tubing. When the heated fluid from the collector flows through these coils, it gives up or *exchanges* its heat to the water stored in the tank. The fluid is then pumped back to the solar collectors for reheating by the sun. This is called a *closed loop* system; the fluid in the collector loop never comes into direct contact with the water in the storage tank. This type of system is suggested wherever there is a need to guard against corrosion, as with aluminum collectors, and where freezing weather occurs. In these cases, an antifreeze mixture with corrosion inhibitors, similar to those used in automobiles, is sometimes recommended for the solar collector portion of the loop. Plain water is used in the storage tank.

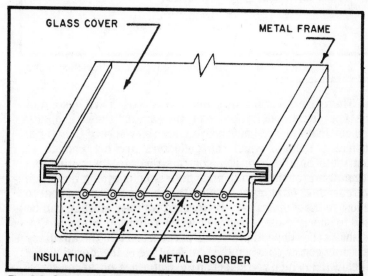

GLASS COVER   METAL FRAME

INSULATION   METAL ABSORBER

Fig. 2-2. Solar collector assembly, flat plate type. The absorber is in a frame with insulation on the back and covered with one pane of glass.

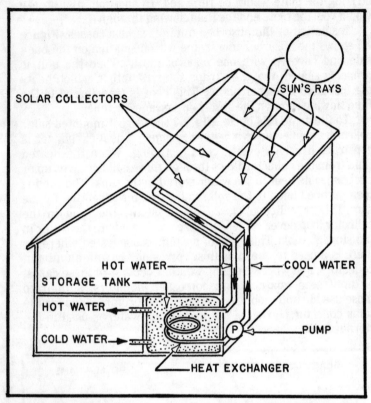

Fig. 2-3. Operating cycle using flat plate collectors, a circulating pump, and a heat exchanger.

There are several valves and controls used in a system of this type; for simplicity, however, they are not shown in detail. You can learn more about their function as you read Chapter 3. Basically, though, when the collectors are hot enough to contribute heat to storage, controls operate the pump and circulate water through them. There is no pumping action on overcast days or at night because this would only cause heat to be lost to the atmosphere. The heated water in storage can be used to supply most of your hot water requirements, and Fig. 2-4 shows the connection for this purpose. Again, the auxiliary heat only comes on when the temperature of the stored water is below that which you select on the water heater thermostat.

For space heating or room heating, Fig. 2-5 shows how the heated water from storage is circulated through the coils of a

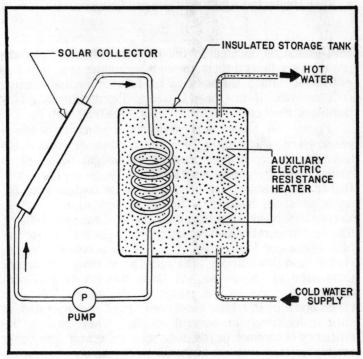

Fig. 2-4. Closed loop heat-exchange system with an auxiliary heat source.

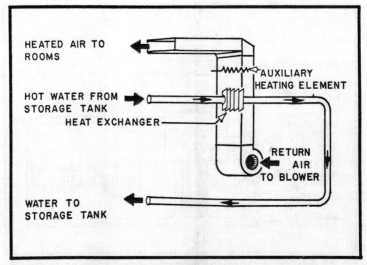

Fig. 2-5. One method of using solar-heated water to provide space or room heating.

heat exchanger located in the forced-air furnace. As the heated water flows through the coils it radiates heat, which is distributed through the house by the furnace fan and existing duct network. If this heat is not sufficient, the auxiliary heating element comes into play to boost the temperature.

Figure 2-6 shows a heat-driven cooling system. A gas-powered refrigerator or air conditioner uses this technology. Since heat is provided by the gas flame, solar cooling merely requires substitution of hot water for the flame. Higher temperatures are needed for solar cooling than for water or space heating. If the water temperature in the storage tank reaches approximately 190°F, it can be channeled into the refrigeration unit, which provides chilled fluid for the heat exchanger located above the furnace blower. As the chilled fluid flows through the coils, a fan blows air across them. The air is cooled and flows through conventional distribution ducts to the rooms in the house. Solar air conditioners of this type have been tested and operated at various locations for several months. They stretch the efficiency of common or flat-plate solar collectors', providing the higher temperatures required to effectively operate an absorption-type cooling unit; marginal performance results if recommended temperatures are not reached. Solar-assisted

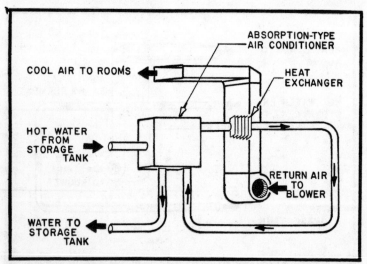

Fig. 2-6. Air conditioning using solar-heated water to drive an absorption-type cooling unit.

heat pumps can also provide cooling, and these are described in Chapter 4.

ALTERNATIVE SYSTEMS

The "working fluid" just described need not be a liquid—it can be *air*. In this case, the unit would be referred to as an *air system*. Systems using a liquid heat transfer are called *hydronic*. Most applications for an air system involve space heating or room heating, as opposed to air conditioning or water heating. As with the hydronic system, you still need a collector, a means of heat storage, a control system, and an auxiliary energy source; but as the warm air is used directly and will not freeze, no separate heat exchangers or antifreeze solutions are required. Rocks or gravel are the most common materials used for heat storage in air systems.

Figure 2-7 illustrates the air-system operation. Air flows over the metal absorber, picking up heat trapped by the glass cover. This heated air is then circulated through the air ducts

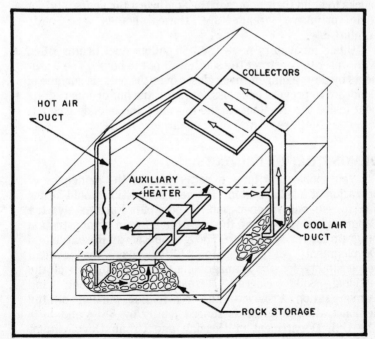

Fig. 2-7. A room heating system using solar-heated air, rock storage, a circulating blower, and an auxiliary heater.

into the rooms, if heat is needed. If heat is not needed, the air is diverted into the storage area where it heats the rocks. This "stored" heat may then be used during periods when sunshine is not available, such as in cloudy weather, at night, or in the early morning. To retrieve the heat, air is blown through the rocks, picking up the stored heat. An auxiliary heater warms the air as required to meet the setting on your thermostat.

Another concept you will hear about is the *passive* system. Simply stated, if you rely on the basic building materials from which the house is constructed to store heat during the day and release it at night, you have a passive system. Those systems where fluid or air is forced to circulate by pumps or blowers are *active*. Passive systems rely on such materials as stones, bricks, adobe blocks, or concrete blocks to absorb heat and hold it for an extended period of time. They work best in desert-type climates, where the days are hot and the nights cold. Generally, they rely on the south wall of the house to collect and store heat. The Pueblo Indians have used adobe blocks to build their homes in the Southwest for years, and for their primitive architecture theses homes are quite comfortable.

Other innovators have used 55-gallon steel drums filled with water to construct the south wall of the home. The water heats by day; a hinged cover closes over the outside surface of the drum to prevent heat loss. At night, the hot drums radiate heat inside the dwelling. In the morning, the outside cover is lowered so the drums may once again store heat.

DEMONSTRATION PROJECTS

You should now have a better idea of the principles of operation of a solar system. My next suggestion would be for you to see one in operation, if possible. Fortunately, the Congress has recognized the need for a broad demonstration program for residential use. Though the Energy Research and Development Administration (ERDA) has the overall responsibility for the management and coordination of the National Solar Energy Research, Development, and Demonstration Program, the residential portion of the demonstration program is shared jointly by ERDA and HUD. The U.S. Department of Housing and Urban Development (HUD) is presently working with manufacturers, developers, and builders to provide residential demonstrations in which

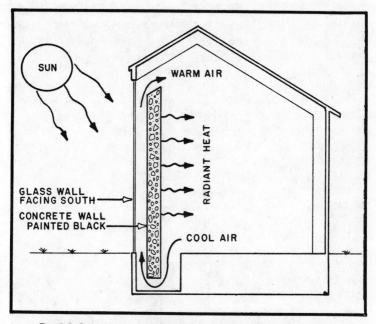

Fig. 2-8. Solar heater (passive-type) with natural air circulation.

solar energy equipment will be installed in both new and existing dwellings.

Accurate records of initial- and operating-costs of the solar systems will be kept and made available to prospective purchasers. Analysis of this data will help the consumer decide if reduced fuel bills are worth the greater initial cost of a solar heating system. The commercial demonstration program, plus the research and development of solar space heating and water heating, as well as solar cooling systems, is under the specific management of ERDA .

The first projects will concentrate on space heating and hot water applications; later ones will involve combined solar heating/cooling systems. A multitude of demonstration projects of this nature have begun to spring up all over the United States, and many more will be constructed throughout the program.

In addition to federally sponsored projects, there are many state and private projects planned or already in use. It is estimated that over 200 solar heated buildings exist today; a college or university in your area may be able to help you

Fig. 2-9. Sugarmill Woods solar residence, Homosassa Springs, Florida.

locate one nearby. Here are a few examples of selected demonstration projects, both privately and federally funded, in the residential and institutional areas.

Sugarmill Woods

The Sugarmill Woods solar house (Fig. 2-9) is located in Homosassa Springs, Forida and was designed by Burt, Hill & Associates, architects for Parkland Properties, Inc. This home demonstrates the use of solar energy for residential heating and cooling in a warm, humid climate. The solar system is expected to handle the entire requirement for domestic hot water, and approximately 60% or more of the air-conditioning needs. The heating needs for the living space and swimming pool will also be supplied by solar energy. Nine hundred square feet of solar collectors are mounted on the garage roof, tilted 14° from the horizontal and oriented 17° west of south. A mechanical room adjacent to the garage contains the 900-gallon water storage tank. The collector tilt and orientation were chosen to optimize heat production on hot summer afternoons, when the highest cooling loads occur. The solar energy will be used to provide space cooling by the use of a hot-water fired, absorption chiller. Heat exchangers are used in the heating modes for domestic hot water and the swimming pool.

Farquier High School

There are two public school projects funded by the National Science Foundation that have interesting features. The Farquier High School in Warrenton, Virginia (Fig. 2-10) is receiving from the sun all of the heat required to meet heating loads of five mobile classrooms (see Fig. 2-11). The operating cost to the school for solar heat is approximately 45¢ per day, representing the cost of electricity to operate the pumps and controls. The solar heating system consists of 2500 sq ft of collectors and two 5500-gallon tanks to store the heated water. The storage system was sized to meet the heat loads of the classrooms for a minimum of 12 days without sunshine under average winter conditions. The total heated room area is 4100 sq ft. The collector mounting, a specially constructed scaffold adjacent to the school, was oriented due south and tilted 53° to the horizontal. This angle was selected to provide the maximum winter heating capability for the Warrenton area. (An 80-page booklet describing the Farquier County Public

Fig. 2-10. Solar collectors for Farquier High School, Warrenton, Virginia. (Courtesy InterTechnology Corp.)

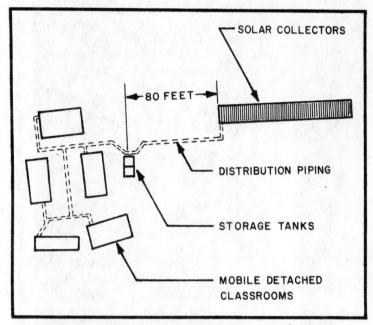

SOLAR COLLECTORS

80 FEET

DISTRIBUTION PIPING

STORAGE TANKS

MOBILE DETACHED
CLASSROOMS

Fig. 2-11. Overhead view of solar layout for Farquier High School.

High School project may be obtained by writing: National Technical Information Service, U.S. Department of Commerce, Washington, D.C. 20230. Request document number NSF-RA-N-74-019.)

Towns Elementary School

The second school, George A. Towns Elementary School in Atlanta, Georgia, is the first demonstration of its kind to use solar energy for both heating and cooling applications. The school drew national attention in the fall of 1975 when its dedication was televised for network news programs. The prime contractor for the system's equipment that provides the solar space heating, water heating, and powering of the solar cooling was Westinghouse. The system uses commercially available components, including a 100-ton absorption cooling machine, 10,000 sq ft of solar collectors, and 11,000 sq ft of reflector panels, making it the largest solar collection installation in the world. It is estimated that it will provide more than 60% of the heating and 80% of the domestic hot water requirements of the school.

Fig. 2-12. The world's largest solar heating and cooling installation is at the George A. Towns Elementary School in Atlanta, Georgia.

PPG Industries, Inc. was a subsystem contractor, supplying the collector panel assembly. The panels, coated with the Alcoa selective surface to improve their efficiency, are mounted in 12 rows on the roof of the building (Fig. 2-12). Flat reflectors, consisting of aluminized Mylar and mounted on a Masonite board, were chosen. These reflectors slope toward the collectors as shown in Fig. 2-13. Their purpose is to focus more energy on the solar collectors, providing an estimated 30% gain in radiation. Three underground tanks are used, totaling 45,000 gallons of storage capacity. The school has an area of 32,000 sq ft to be heated and cooled. This type of building is well suited for solar operation, as it is occupied mainly during daylight hours. (Operating data on the Towns School project is now starting to become available, and also may be obtained from the National Technical Information Service.)

Columbus House

I had suggested that you might contact your nearest university for information regarding solar energy display homes. If you do, you may be surprised to discover one right on its campus. Ohio State University at Columbus, in cooperation with the Ohio Exposition Center, has located its Columbus House on the Ohio State Fairgrounds (Fig. 2-14). The design is typically that of a new Midwestern home: one-story elevation, four bedrooms, two and a half baths, a basement, and a two-car garage adjacent to the house. The total living area that is heated is 2200 sq ft. Architecturally, many energy-saving ideas have been implemented, including the use of small windows called *vision strips*. Both the walls and roof are well insulated.

Also featured are three unheated *atriums*, interior enclosed tropical courtyards, which total in area 600 sq ft. These are covered by transparent roofs, and ventilation is provided. Thirty-seven panels, made by PPG Industries, make up the 800 sq ft of flat plate collectors (Fig. 2-15). They are located in three sections of roof, sloping at 45°. The glass used for the panels is double glazed; the nonselective coating is a black enamel. The collector fluid is a mixture of water and ethylene glycol, with two 2000-gallon tanks providing heat storage. A heat pump is employed to assist the solar heating,

Fig. 2-13 View of solar collectors (on left) with augmentation by reflectors.

Fig. 2-14. Columbus House, Columbus, Ohio. (Courtesy PPG Industries.)

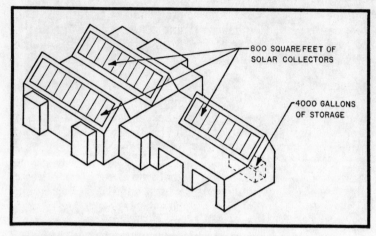

Fig. 2-15. Location of collectors and storage tanks on Columbus House.

and it is also used as a backup to the cooling system. It is anticipated that 50% to 70% of the heat required for the house, including heat for household water, will be supplied by this solar system.

During the summer, the house is cooled by an absorption system using lithium bromide and water. This system is powered by heat from the storage tanks, using an auxiliary electric heater or heat pump.

The Columbus House project is a joint venture of Ohio State University and the Homewood Corporation.

Ouroboros-East

The University of Minnesota, at Minneapolis, has two demonstration projects. Those of you who are thinking of adding solar heat to an older home will be interested in the University's Ouroboros-East house at St. Paul. Built in 1910, this two-story house was made available by HUD in 1974. The 2000 sq ft house also has a basement and an attic. Installing a solar heating system in an older structure such as this requires some alterations to accommodate the system, and necessitates adding good-quality insulation.

The flat plate collector (water type) was installed in two sections. A 600 sq ft portion was mounted on a roof, sloping at 45°; 500 sq ft was mounted on the vertical south wall. Water is pumped upward behind double glazing, into the space between two sheets of galvanized steel. A 2000-gallon cylindrical steel storage tank was placed horizontally in the basement. The rooms are heated by hot air, using a heat exchanger and a blower. Both this and the Ouroboros-South house are projects of the School of Architecture and Landscape Architecture.

Ouroboros-South

Ouroboros-South, in Rosemount, is the more exciting of the two houses. Its very appearance is dramatic, having a trapezoid-design floor plan, with the south wall rising two stories to collect the sun's heat through spacious windows and mirror-like collector panels (see Fig. 2-16). The house is sheltered by a sod-covered roof that tapers to a low, narrow north wall. The sod cover provides additional insulation, allowing an accumulation of snow during the winter and cooling by evaporation in the summer (Fig. 2-17).

The 2000 sq ft house is designed with the idea of being as self-sufficient as possible. Some of its energy conserving experiments include such features as a closed-cycle composting toilet, Japanese-style furo (soaking tub), fine mist showers and faucets that minimize the use of water, and a windmill. Nine inches of insulation were used in the walls, and earth berms cover most of the north wall and half of the east-west walls. The building is designed to capture cool summer breezes for natural air conditioning.

Fig. 2-16. Ouroboros-South house, Rosemont, Minnesota.

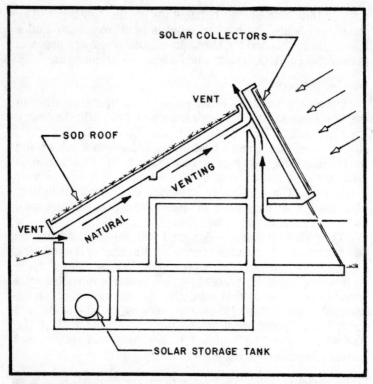

Fig. 2-17. Cross section of Ouroboros-South house, showing natural venting for summer cooling.

In the beginning, the solar collection was accomplished entirely by a *trickling water* collector, made of corrugated galvanized steel between two sheets of glass, with water running down the valleys of the galvanized steel. On a sunny day, the water becomes 20° to 50°F hotter, enters a gutter, and flows by way of the water preheater to the 1000-gallon storage tank in the basement. The cylindrical steel container is surrounded by 50 tons of fist-size stones. A conventional forced-air system draws heated air from these stones and sends it to the rooms.

In order to solve a heat transfer problem, mechanical engineer John Ilse designed a new collector, which is now positioned alternately across the roof with the original open-trickle collector panels. In the internal-flow steel Sandwich Panel collector (patents pending), which is now being commercially marketed by Ilse, the water flows between two sheets of lightweight dimpled steel that have been spot-welded together, similar to the construction shown in Fig. 2-18. The open edges are sealed, with pipe fittings installed at the ends. A coating is applied, and the panels are covered with glass. A pump is used to raise the water from the storage tank to a space at the bottom of the collector. The fluid then flows upward between the sandwiched metal sheets, picking up the sun's heat. At the top of the collector, the fluid drains back into the storage tank below. Because the cooling water reaches the entire inner surface of the panel, the heat transfer is highly

Fig. 2-18. Dimpled steel absorber Sandwich Panel (patents pending) used in the Ilse Engineering solar collector.

efficient. In addition, heat loss from the humid air being in contact with the glass cover has been reduced by completely enclosing the panel. Data is constantly being gathered on the collectors for later evaluation.

The Energy House

The idea of using a showcase to demonstrate the dual concepts of solar energy used in conjunction with energy-conservation features has produced still another project drawing public attention. Located at Quechee, Vermont, the Energy House was specifically designed to fit the means of the middle-income homeowner (Fig. 2-19). Its spacious 2100 sq ft allows for all the conveniences that are so much a part of today's living. The realization of this project is due to the cooperation and combined efforts of Blue/Sun Ltd. of Farmington, Connecticut, architect; Terrosi Construction Inc. of Quechee, Vermont, builder; and Grumman Aerospace Corporation, Bethpage, New York, solar-system designer and supplier of the solar collectors. A responsible land developer, Quechee Lakes Corporation was determined that the Energy House project would strictly adhere to the environmental standards and the expected high quality in design appearance. Careful study of the availability and costs of the energy sources in that area resulted in a design using a solar water-to-air heat pump system with an auxiliary oil burner. (Natural gas was not available; and though both electric baseboard heating and oil heating were used, the costs of the electricity had several different rate schedules, depending on the kind of system used.)

The purpose of the solar system was to provide space heating and domestic hot water to the residence. The average summer temperatures of the area are around 65°F, and there is a prevailing summer wind; thus the cooling could be accomplished by making use of natural breezes rather than air conditioning. That prevailing wind is 20° west of south so, after it was determined that moving the house 20° from the south would have little effect on the collection of the sun's rays, that was the selected orientation of the house. Sixteen Grumman Sunstream 50A solar collectors, totaling 400 sq ft, are mounted in two sections of the 45° sloping roof (see Fig. 2-19). Since the site of the house is approximately 43.5° north latitude, an angle of 55° for the roof would ordinarily have been indicated for maximum solar collection during the winter. But from an

Fig. 2-19. The Energy Houses in Quechee Vermont. (Courtesy Grumman Energy Programs.)

architectural viewpoint, it was contended that angles greater than 45° would only result in an undesirable use of space within the house. It was also demonstrated that the performance of the collectors would not show any appreciable difference by slanting the roof to 45°. It is estimated that this system will provide 40% to 50% of the heating requirements of the residence.

In comparing the Quechee project house with a standard-construction house employing the same solar collector system, the analysis concluded that only 20% of the energy needs would be met in the latter. This, indeed, should serve to point out the importance of incorporating various energy-conserving measures into the design of the home. In addition to using a high-quality insulation in the Quechee house, the walls were specially sealed against air infiltration. Triple-glazed windows were used on three sides of the building, no windows being installed on the northern exposure. An entry hall minimizes heat lost from opening and closing the outside door; a solarium gathers heat during the day, and is equipped with special shutters to prevent its escape at night; the fireplace is fitted with a glass screen to provide a net heat gain to the house. Even the site of the house is important. It is located near a line of trees that serve as a barrier to the winter wind. Because of these added features, the Quechee Energy House realized the better return on its investment from the same solar collectors used in the standard-construction home. In a cost comparison with conventional heating systems, (Fig. 2-20), the Quechee home was found to have the lowest cost option, and its system payback period was estimated to be 4½ years.

Our discussion of demonstration residences would not be complete without mentioning the homes of Dr. Harry E. Thomason, J. D. An innovator and builder, Thomason has a long involvement with solar energy for home applications. His designs, many of which carry extensive patent protection, have been used in several houses in the Washington, D. C. area since 1959. The Thomason *Solaris* system has a basic, uncomplicated approach to solar collection, using a sloped south roof as the collector—the trickling-water idea. Water trickles down the valleys of corrugated aluminum, painted flat-black and covered by glazed panes, and into a basement storage tank that is the heart of the Solaris system. The

COST COMPARISON WITH CONVENTIONAL SYSTEMS

Item	Electric Heating and Hot Water	Oil Heating and Electric Hot Water	Quechee House System
Int'l Investment	$1500	$1750	$7000
Mortgage (30 Yr at 8.5%)	$ 139	$ 163	$ 650
Maintenance	Assumed Negligible	$ 50	$ 100
Heating Costs			
—Electric	$1681	—	$ 245†
—Oil	—	$ 648	$ 218
Energy Usage			
For Heating			
—KWh	47,875	—	6676
—Gal	—	1620	540
Hot Water System			
—Cost	$ 163	$163	$ 90
—KWh	8900	8,900	3750
Total Annual Cost	$1983	$1024	$1303
Annual Operating Cost	$1844	$ 861	$ 653

† Includes $69 for fan and pump operation

Fig. 2-20. Economic analysis of the Quechee Energy House, estimating the payback of the initial investment at 4½ years. The comparison is for a house with standard insulation.

cylindrical steel tank (which holds anywhere from 1500 to 3000 gallons of water in the different homes) is surrounded by 25 to 50 tons of stones. Heat from this container is sent through the rest of the house by means of a simple low-power hot air system.

Thomason has eliminated the need for a furnace on the Solaris systems and, by reducing the ductwork, has further lowered costs. No valves or dampers are used on the system, thus adding to the inventor's claim of simplicity and economy. And only one thermostat is used to control the heat collection and activate the summer air conditioning. For air-conditioning purposes, the system stores and dehumidifies cool night air, making use of a small compressor and the same blower used for the system's heat distribution.

Colorado State University

Another forerunner in solar heating systems is G. O. G. Lof of Colorado State University. As early as 1945, Professor George Lof was experimenting with solar heating systems. His

Fig. 2-21. Colorado State University Solar House.

system in the Lof house in Denver, built in 1959, remains in use today. Under the direction of solar engineers Lof and D. S. Ward, Colorado State University at Fort Collins boasts of three solar houses, each similar in architectural design, but using different types of collectors.

House I (Fig. 2-21) utilizes a water-type collector made of an aluminum sheet, with integral expanded channels and a nonselective coating. The double-strength glass is double glazed. Although no antifreeze was added to the water, it does contain a corrosion inhibitor.

An air-type collector was used for House II. Galvanized steel with a nonselective black coating was chosen here. A blower circulates the air through the space beneath the galvanized steel and carries it to a storage bin of stones. Air blown through the stones brings heat to the house as required.

House III demonstrates an entirely different method of collection. A steel tank located in the basement serves as the storage container, as in House I. But the solar collector is made up of long glass tubes arranged in parallel fashion. Each tube contains a strip of copper attached to a copper tube. A selective coating has been applied in this instance, and the fluid used is a mixture of water and antifreeze.

As pointed out in Chapter 1, geographical area is an important factor to consider when deciding on an investment in a solar system. The area around Denver was shown to be ideal for solar collection, so it is not surprising to find so many excellent examples of solar energy being used for the heating and cooling of private residences. In addition, the regional architecture, with its chalet-type roofs and advanced styles, facilitates the task of integrating collector panels into the house design. An earnest effort should be made to achieve a pleasing appearance in the installation of a solar system.

The Denver firm of Crowther, Kruse, and McWilliams was responsible for the architectural design of the Colorado State University solar houses. The Crowther Solar Group, which specializes in energy-optimized architectural concepts, can point with pride to several completed and current projects. The private residences that are now occupied are being monitored by the Public Service Company of Colorado.

Cherry Creek

Cherry Creek, in Denver, is a solar project of architect Richard L. Crowther that demonstrates a retrofit house plus

Fig. 2-22. Cherry Creek solar residences, Denver, Colorado. This view is from the north side of the dwellings.

the addition of a newly constructed home on the same lot. The front unit, at the left in Fig. 2-22, is the result of extensively remodeling an older stucco bungalow for energy conservation and solar collection. The 1100 sq ft dwelling sports a completely new exterior, refinished with stucco and cedar shake shingles on the roof and sidewalls. The interior was modernized, and energy-saving features were included wherever possible. An old basement coalbin was converted to a heat storage area with open concrete-block flooring and filled with 20 cu yd of large-size gravel. A newly insulated north wall, running the length of the house, protects it from chilling winter winds. The south roof was modified to a 53° angle for the most effective use of the solar collector (Fig. 2-23). The collector is a flat plate air-type, with ⅛ in. thick cover plates and a flat-black coating. Figure 2-23 shows a reinforced gutter and top member, supporting a movable ladder for easy access to the collector. The reinforced units also act as a snow trap.

The rear unit is a 2000 sq ft residence designed as a prototype for either on-site or modular construction for townhouses, cluster housing, or single-family use. The flat plate collector, in this instance a water type, is also mounted on a south roof, sloping at 53°. The design of this home is a square, three-level stacking plan, with two bedrooms, spacious closets, bathroom, a utility room, a multipurpose room, and a greenhouse making up the lower level. Since the ideal sleeping temperatures are considered to be between 62° and 65°F, less heating and cooling is needed for the bedrooms, situated as they are below grade.

The greenhouse (Fig. 2-24), with its clear Plexiglas double-glazed insulating panels, performs like a solar collector. A glass-enclosed space above it also holds a water-type solar collector that circulates heated water into a 380-gallon fiberglass tank. Controlled evaporation is provided to humidify the greenhouse, and a duct to the furnace sends humidity throughout the house during the winter. Being below grade, the insulated greenhouse takes advantage of earth-temperature thermal inertia, and heat loss is minimized. Sliding glass doors can be opened, allowing the solar heat and humidity to directly warm the lower level rooms. Summer cooling is accomplished by an evaporative cooler and turbine-fan exhaust system situated on the roof, visible in Fig. 2-24.

Fig. 2-23. Southeast corner of Cherry Creek residence showing solar collectors. Also note the reinforced gutter and top member.

Fig. 2-24. Greenhouse on rear unit of Cherry Creek complex.

The Pinery

The Pinery, shown in prototype (Fig. 2-25), is a spacious 3800 sq ft residence set in the pine woods near Pinery, Colorado. A 585 sq ft air-type flat plate collector is used to supply the energy for this three-level home. The Crowther Solar Group has included many energy-optimization features in its design: positioning the garage and earth berms as a buffer against cold northwest winds and to minimize heat loss; using heavy cedar shake shingles and 12 inches of roof insulation; adding double-door airlock entries; double glazing the recessed southern-exposure windows and reflective glazing the western-exposure windows. Natural ventilation provides the summer cooling. It is expected that the energy-conserving features and the solar system will take care of 80% of the home's space heating needs and 50% of the cooling needs.

Santa Clara

On July 4, 1975, the city of Santa Clara dedicated its new Community Recreation Building. (See Fig. 2-26 for the architect's rendering of this building.) The 27,000 sq ft multipurpose building in Central Park features an adobe-colored exterior with red roof tiles, blending beautifully into the quiet Spanish atmosphere of this California community. It is among the first buildings in the world to use solar energy for both heating and cooling. The system is expected to save $5000 worth of gas annually at current prices, and it is anticipated that it will supply 75% to 80% of the heating and cooling needs for the building.

Over half of the roof surface is covered by collector panels. These are double-glazed, flat plate collectors, using copper absorber plates with a selective coating. Water passes through the panels and is heated to over $200°F$. This hot water is used for the cooling process as well as the heating. For heating, the hot water passes through a heat exchanger, where the heat is transferred to the water through fan/coil units. Similar to those used for conventional heating and cooling systems, these units provide warm air to the building. For cooling purposes, the hot water from the collectors furnishes the energy to work the water chillers, which cool the water flowing through separate coils of the same fan/coil units. Thus cool air is provided for distribution by the forced-air system. A

Fig. 2-25. A model of the Pinery, a suburban community residence near Denver, Colorado, using an air-type solar collector.

Fig. 2-26. Architect's rendering of Santa Clara Community Recreation Building. Santa Clara, California.

fresh-air economizer cycle was added to mix in air from the outside whenever needed.

Underground pipes carry the water to hot and cold storage tanks buried outside the perimeter of the building. Computerized tests have shown that storing the cold water separately provides a 10% decrease in gas usage when compared to a system that stores only hot water. Additionally, the cold water storage offered a significant capital cost savings. A backup system (a gas-fired boiler) is provided, and automatic controls select which parts of the solar and auxiliary systems are to be used in response to the required room temperatures in the different areas of the multipurpose center.

SUMMARY

In taking you along on this "reader's tour" of solar demonstration projects and applications, I have attempted to provide you with a brief look at a variety of systems, some different types of buildings, both commercial and residential, and a geographical cross section of building locations. You should keep in mind, when appraising these and other solar demonstrations, that some of them were designed to test certain systems. Some will, naturally, be more costly or less efficient than you might require for your own home. The importance of this survey is to point out the ever-growing interest in solar energy and the wide scope of solar heating and cooling applications in the United States today.

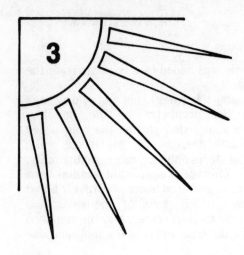

3

System Components

Once the decision to invest in a solar heater is made, it may be a frustrating experience to sort out the type of system best suited to your individual needs. There are air systems and water systems, rock storage and water storage, flat plate collectors and concentrating collectors from which to choose, plus new concepts presently under development. This chapter provides the basic options available. The knowledge of how these individual components operate is essential in intelligent system selection.

COLLECTOR PANELS

The heart of any solar system is the *collector panel*. Not only does it represent as much as 50% of the system's materials cost, but its efficiency is the key to economical operation.

First, consider *flat plate* collectors, as opposed to the *focusing* or *reflector* type. The term *flat plate* is used almost universally in the industry, describing collectors having absorbers that are basically of a flat configuration. This type of collector is the most popular. It can operate on diffuse, or scattered, radiation available on hazy days, in addition to being able to operate in direct sunlight. The *reflector* type, on the other hand, requires bright sunshine to operate effectively, and it would not be suitable in areas with a high percentage of diffuse radiation.

The flat plate construction, shown in Fig. 2-2, may use various types of absorber plates made of aluminum, copper, steel, black plastic, or a combination of these materials.

ABSORBERS

The primary function of the *absorber* is to capture as much of the solar radiation reaching it as possible, and transfer its energy as heat to the heat transfer medium. To do this efficiently requires material with good thermal conductivity, and a design to minimize the distance the collected heat must travel to reach the heat transfer medium. The property of thermal conductivity is less important when air is used as the transfer medium, due to greater flow rates and the overall transfer surface area. The heat transfer medium, whether air or liquid, is either contained in tubeways (or channels) within the absorber or allowed to flow over its surface.

Aluminum Absorber

Figures 3-1 through 3-4 illustrate several different concepts using a *liquid* heat transfer medium. Each of these designs is conceived by its inventor to be the ultimate in solar collection. The fact is that each design has both advantages and disadvantages. The extruded aluminum tube with integral fins (Fig. 3-1) should be used only in a closed loop system, with inhibitors in the transfer liquid to guard against corrosion. It is an economical means of fabricating an absorber, however, as the "fins" may be cut away from the tube wherever return bends are needed, and the material may be folded back on itself or be "serpentined" to the size of absorber that is needed. Some test results indicate that placing the tubes in a serpentine pattern, rather than using headers to connect parallel tubes, provides a greater temperature rise for the same area.

A greater pressure drop (more pumping power) must be expected with this design. And care must be taken to run the tubes horizontally when the collector is installed to prevent trapped fluid when draining, either for freeze protection or fluid replacement. Another advantage of the serpentine pattern is the elimination of tube connections within the absorber, reducing the possibility of leaks.

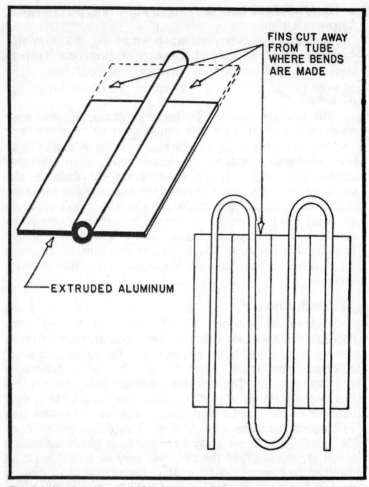

FINS CUT AWAY
FROM TUBE
WHERE BENDS
ARE MADE

EXTRUDED ALUMINUM

Fig. 3-1. An absorber made from an extruded aluminum tube having integral fins. The extrusion is bent to form a serpentine pattern.

Bimetallic Absorber

Bimetallic absorbers (Fig. 3-2) normally use aluminum sheets with copper tubes soldered or mechanically attached to them. The tubes can either take a serpentine pattern or be connected with headers. Copper alone has been used for many years to carry household water with good results; it is expensive, however. With this aluminum-copper combination, the aluminum transfers heat economically to the copper.

Joining metals requires considerable skill to achieve a good *thermal bond* across the joint. Without such a bond, a substantial amount of heat efficiency is lost. Be sure the product has a good bond and that performance data is provided to back up the manufacturer's claims. A securely soldered tube can transfer as much as 300 times more heat across the joint than one that has been poorly soldered; but if solder is used, the absorber temperatures should never exceed the melting point of the solder.

The use of rectangular, square, or oval tubes, rather than round ones, provides more surface area in contact with the absorber sheet and can increase heat transfer if thermal bonds are of good quality. When a mechanical attachment is made, heat-conducting filler materials are generally used between the metal parts. For example, in Fig. 3-2 a filler of paste-like

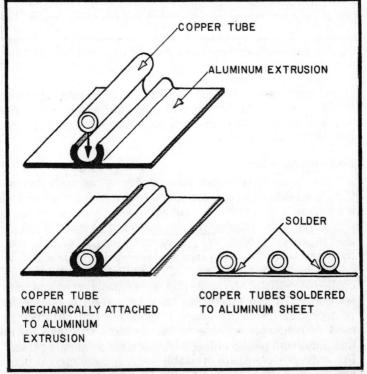

COPPER TUBE

ALUMINUM EXTRUSION

SOLDER

COPPER TUBE
MECHANICALLY ATTACHED
TO ALUMINUM
EXTRUSION

COPPER TUBES SOLDERED
TO ALUMINUM SHEET

Fig. 3-2. Two concepts of attaching copper tubes to aluminum: mechanically attached or soldered.

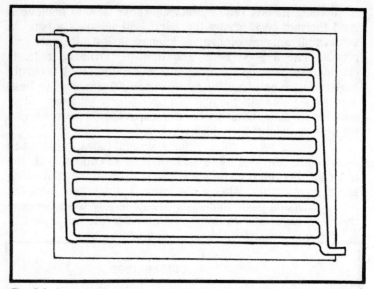

Fig. 3-3. A sandwich absorber panel, made by the Olin Brass Roll-Bond process.

consistency between the copper tube and aluminum extrusion would fill in irregular or void areas and improve heat transfer. This also reduces the chances of moisture collecting between the metals and causing corrosion.

Sandwich Absorber

The sandwich absorber panel in Fig. 3-3 is made by the Olin Brass Roll-Bond process. To make this panel, one sheet of aluminum or copper is silk-screened with a pattern representing the tubular passages desired. A special ink is used to prevent bonding in the patterned areas. A back sheet of the same material is put into place, and the "sandwich" is heated and rolled together. After rolling, air pressure is applied to "inflate" the areas that were silk-screened and thus not bonded. These assemblies have been used in household refrigerators for many years. If an aluminum absorber is used, corrosion protection must be provided. An advantage is that aluminum panels of this design are economically priced. For water heaters where drinkable water is circulated, copper absorbers should be used. All-copper sandwich panels are only available in smaller sizes and at higher costs.

Another concept, shown in Fig. 3-4, allows water to flow by gravity down the grooves or channels in a piece of corrugated sheet metal. This is a simple method that works well in specific geographic regions. It is low in cost, but a loss of efficiency can occur, due to condensation on the glass that covers the absorber or mineral deposits on the painted surface of the sheet.

Plastic Absorber

Plastic is also used as an absorber material, with solar swimming-pool heaters being the most common application. Plastic is generally lower in cost than metal and has better corrosion resistance. It does have some limitations, however, such as low operating temperatures, low thermal conductivity, and high expansion and contraction. Some types of plastic degrade rapidly under intense sunlight, so be sure to investigate the grade and specifications of plastic used. There

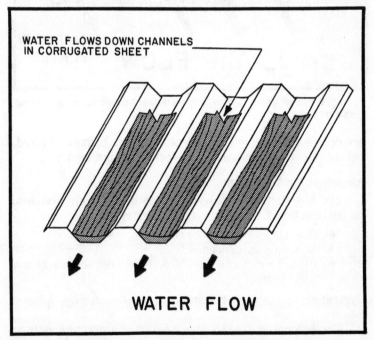

WATER FLOWS DOWN CHANNELS IN CORRUGATED SHEET

WATER FLOW

Fig. 3-4. An open-flow system using a corrugated sheet-metal absorber. Gravity forces the water down the grooves or channels in the corrugated sheet metal.

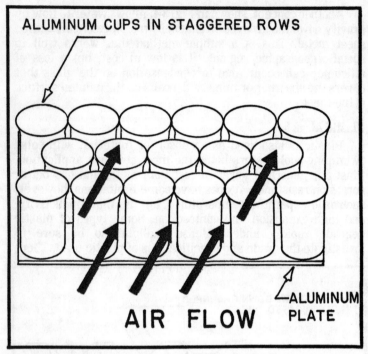

ALUMINUM CUPS IN STAGGERED ROWS

AIR FLOW

ALUMINUM PLATE

Fig. 3-5. A system using airflow to transfer heat collected by staggered aluminum cups.

are dozens of additional designs of absorbers being evaluated, but the most common ones use the principles outlined here.

Absorbers for Air Systems

For a system used only for space heating, air systems, rather than liquid, present several advantages. These are:

- There is less chance for corrosion.
- No antifreeze is needed.
- Heated air can be used directly without the need for a heat exchanger.

Typical absorbers for air systems are shown in Figs. 3-5 and 3-6.

The concept in Fig. 3-5 uses a series of aluminum cups in staggered rows, with air flowing along the sides and over the tops of the cups. This design claims higher efficiency as a result of a greater absorber area.

In Fig. 3-6, a corrugated sheet-metal absorber has air flowing over its surface. This type of absorber has the potential of economical performance, if properly designed. Although Fig. 3-6 shows one type of corrugation, it is possible to modify the shape not only to take advantage of a specific orientation to the sun, but to capture some of the long-wave radiation emitted from a hot absorber surface. This emitted energy may intercept an adjacent corrugation and reduce the overall heat losses from the absorber. A disadvantage of air is that it cannot be used economically for hot water or cooling applications.

SELECTIVE ABSORBER COATINGS

An improvement in efficiency can be obtained by applying a *selective* coating to that portion of the absorber exposed to sunlight. After sunlight strikes the absorber, part of the energy is reradiated from the surface as long-wave or infrared radiation. A selective coating combines high solar *absorptivity* (capacity of material to absorb radiant energy) with low

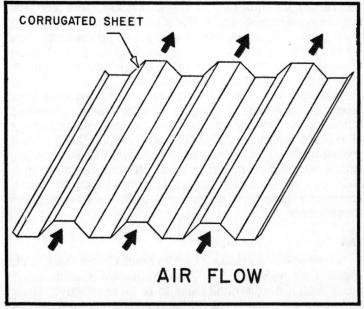

Fig. 3-6. A corrugated sheet-metal absorber using air as heat-transfer medium.

infrared *emittance* (reradiated energy), permitting the absorber to retain more of the sunlight energy striking its surface.

Flat-black paint, which is commonly used on absorbers, is not selective because its absorptivity and emittance are approximately equal. For low-temperature applications, black paint may be suitable; but it is doubtful that the higher temperatures needed to operate a solar air conditioner can be economically achieved without the use of a selective coating. Any collector manufacturer who has "done his homework" will coat the absorber in a manner to obtain maximum performance at a minimum cost with long-term durability.

Advantages of Selective Coatings

Let's further explore the advantages of a selective coating. In general, effective operating temperatures for working fluids are 140°F for space or room heating, 150°F for domestic hot water, and 220°F for absorption-type air conditioning. Colorado State University made a direct comparison between two commercial coatings: 3M Nextel brand Velvet Coating black paint (101-C10) and the Alcoa 655 selective surface. The test results shown in Fig. 3-7 reveal that the Alcoa selective surface was consistently hotter than the 3M black Velvet Coating over the temperature range tested. These tests were under static conditions (no fluid flowing) on 8- by 10-inch specimens that were sealed in a 4 in. deep box covered with ⅛ in. thick glass and rotated to follow the sun.

Although not conclusive, there is good evidence that selective absorber coatings, through their improved efficiency, can provide a reduction in the total square footage of collector surface needed for specific solar heating and cooling applications. Also, tests have shown that an absorber with a selective coating may be as efficient operating in a collector using one cover pane as a two-cover collector with a nonselective absorber. This can result in substantial savings to the consumer.

Choosing a Selective Coating

Other selective coatings, such as Black Chrome and Black Nickel, have been tested by NASA (National Aeronautics and Space Administration) and found to be quite effective. Their cost, however, has precluded widespread commercial use. As all coatings mentioned have only been available for a short time, long-term environmental exposure tests should be conducted to prove their durability and performance for this application.

To summarize, nonselective paints such as 3M black Velvet Coating are perfectly suitable for applications where the emittance of the absorber does not drastically alter the efficiency of the collector. You will see more on efficiency later in the book; but as a general rule, if the temperature difference between the working fluid flowing through the absorber and the outside air is 130°F or greater, a selective coating should be considered. If paints are used, they should be

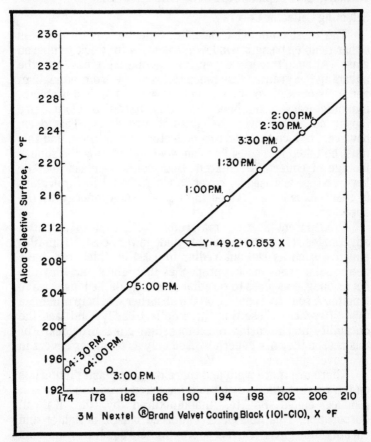

Fig. 3-7. A Colorado State University experiment comparing two absorber coatings.

black in color and formulated to uniformly scatter light without glare or a glossy appearance. They must be properly applied and cured to prevent *outgassing* (a term used to describe vapors from the paint condensing inside the cover panes, causing lower efficiency).

COVER PANES

For acceptable efficiency, the absorber must be covered by one or more transparent *cover panes* that allow short-wave solar radiation to pass through to the absorber but block the reradiated long-wave or infrared energy. Both glass and certain grades of plastic are candidate materials.

Selecting Collector Covers

The most common choice for collector covers today is either double-strength window glass or ⅛ in. thick tempered glass. Although more expensive, tempered glass has the advantage of greater resistance to breakage from vandalism and hailstones. If you live in an area where hail is a problem, manufacturers recommend that ½ in. hardware cloth (wire mesh) be placed over the glass to protect it. This does, however, reduce the *effective* collector area by 10%, and this must be taken into consideration when calculating the square footage of collectors required. Both common glass and the low-iron type are used for cover panes. Although low-iron glass is more expensive, it transmits more solar energy to the absorber.

Transparent-plastic materials offer the potential advantages of lighter weight and lower cost. Thin-film plastics, such as DuPont Tedlar in 0.004 in. thickness, have better solar transmission properties than glass, but they are not as opaque as glass to reradiated energy in the longer wave lengths. A selective coating on the absorber will help minimize this difference. These thin films deflect easily, and lack the durability and abrasion resistance that glass provides. For this reason they are generally used only as the inner covers in two-cover systems.

There are more rigid and more durable plastic materials on the market that are suitable for exterior covers. One is a product called Sunlite, manufactured by the Kalwall Corporation. This fiberglass-reinforced plastic is lighter and cheaper than glass, and has approximately equal transmission qualities. It is not as rigid as glass, however, and must be recoated with resin on a periodic basis.

Another product is Lexan, produced by General Electric. Lexan is lightweight and extremely durable, but it costs more than glass. It is estimated that this product will suffer a 10% transmission loss over a seven-year period due to the effect of ultraviolet degradation. This is a problem that plagues most plastic cover materials.

How Many Cover Panes?

The next question relates to the number of cover panes needed. In General Electric's *Phase 0 Report* (NSF-RA-N-74-021B), prepared for the National Science Foundation, it was concluded that selectively coated absorbers covered with a single pane of ⅛ in. thick water-white glass performed equal to or better than two panes of glass on an absorber coated with flat-black paint. A selectively coated absorber with two cover panes gives even better performance. Other interesting observations were:

- Heat pump systems perform best with single-pane collectors.
- Double-pane collectors are best suited to heat exchange systems, especially in colder northern climates.
- Single-pane collectors may be preferable in less severe southern climates, such as Phoenix or Los Angeles.
- Absorption-type solar air-conditioning systems are best suited for maximum performance with double-pane collectors. Single-pane systems may be a better bargain in southern climates.

As these observations involve various types of system arrangements, I would suggest that you refer back to this information after reading Chapter 4. As a general rule, you can figure that a dual-glazed collector costs 20% more than one with single glazing, so only buy what you need commensurate with the performance required. This subject is discussed further in Chapter 5.

One last comment on cover panes. There are treatments being developed for glass that tend to reflect infrared reradiation from the absorber panel and, at the same time, allow short-wave solar radiation to pass. One process etches the glass in acid; another uses a coating on the inside surface of the glass. In either case, about a 3% reduction in reflection losses have been reported. Both of these methods offer good potential for improving efficiency by reducing reflection. Antireflective glass coatings should be commercialized in the near future.

COLLECTOR HEAT LOSS

The performance of the solar collector can be improved by two major methods:

- Increasing the transfer of energy through the cover and absorber to the working fluid.
- Decreasing the heat losses from the collector to the outside air.

In the previous discussion, increasing the transfer of energy was covered by explaining the need for one or more transparent cover panes to insulate the absorber and hold in the heat. Increasing absorptivity and reducing emittance with selective absorber coatings also improves energy transfer. The design considerations of the absorber itself, and the choice of metals, thickness, bonding, and tube configuration, which all govern the transfer of heat to the flowing liquid, were provided.

This section will explain the ways heat can be lost from the collector and will suggest methods for reducing or decreasing these losses, which occur in three ways:

- Conduction
- Convection
- Radiation

Conductive Losses

Conductive losses occur through the frame, back surface, and cover panes of the collector. As metal absorbers are good conductors of heat, any heat collected by them would be conducted to the metal frame, if there were no insulating material between the surfaces. The length of the arrows in Fig. 3-8 shows the relative losses with or without insulation. A piece of insulating material prevents large amounts of heat from being lost through the frame. With the thermal break, more heat is contained in the absorber and transferred to the working fluid.

The back of the absorber must be insulated to prevent any heat loss through the back of the collector due to conduction. A

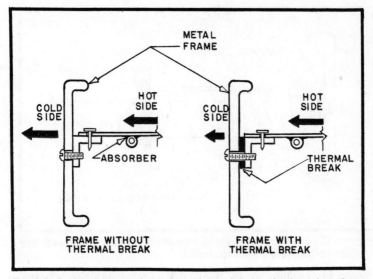

Fig. 3-8. An insulating technique used to minimize the heat loss from edges of the absorber. The length of the arrows shows the relative losses with or without insulation.

combination I would recommend is one inch of fiberglass (next to the absorber) backed by one inch of closed-cell foam, with a reflective aluminum-foil vapor barrier between these surfaces. Common building fiberglass uses a binder material that can cause an odor and outgassing when heated above 250°F. An industrial grade that can handle 400°F temperatures is best, even though it may be more expensive. A cross section of this insulation behind the absorber is shown in Fig. 3-9.

Be sure not to select a design that uses polyurethane foam insulation in direct contact with the absorber. This was done in the ERDA demonstration project at Grover Cleveland School in Boston, resulting in collector failures. The polyurethane foam was unable to withstand the high temperatures without swelling and distorting. Closed-cell urethane foam has an upper-use temperature of approximately 225°F, so you can see why it is not used next to the absorber. Common foamed-plastic insulation that is not of the closed-cell type is not recommended, as it can trap moisture or leaking heat transfer fluid and cause severe problems.

The conduction of heat from the front of the absorber through the air layers between the absorber and cover panes

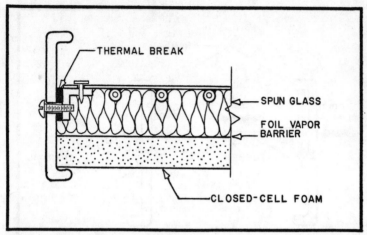

Fig. 3-9. Cross section of suggested insulation to reduce the heat loss from the back surface of the absorber.

also occurs. This can be reduced by increasing the spacing between the absorber and cover; but too much space leads to far greater heat losses by convection.

Convection Losses

Convection is defined as the transfer of heat due to the motion of a liquid or gas. In a solar collector, convective losses can be separated into *internal* losses (from the absorber to the outside cover pane) and *external* losses (from the outside cover pane to the outside air). Convection may also be either *free* or *forced*.

In *free* convection, the movement of the air is caused by a temperature difference. This is what occurs when hot air from the heated absorber rises. A small amount of heat is lost, and the difference in temperature causes a *convection current* to be set up between the absorber and the inside glass cover. The circular path of this flow is illustrated in Fig. 3-10. If there were less air in this area, such as a partial vacuum, this convection would be minimized, and the absorber would retain even more of the heat it generates. A collector having a complete or partial vacuum is expensive to manufacture, and its effective use will be limited to solar air conditioning, where higher temperatures are required.

Forced convection is caused by winds blowing across the outer cover pane. This tends to "sweep" heat away from the outer cover, increasing the temperature differential between that surface and the absorber, and causing more heat to leave the collector.

Studies have shown that the greatest heat loss occurs with the first 10 mph of wind speed. In addition, selectively coated absorbers are much less sensitive to wind-speed variations than those coated with flat-black paint. Some experimental work has been done on reducing convection losses through the use of a honeycomb structure between the absorber and cover pane. This would confine the air to small cells and reduce movement. Based on present technology, high cost and lack of durability at high temperatures are deterrents to this concept.

Radiation Losses

Radiation losses from the absorber can be minimized by using a selective absorber coating. Also, a 3% reduction in

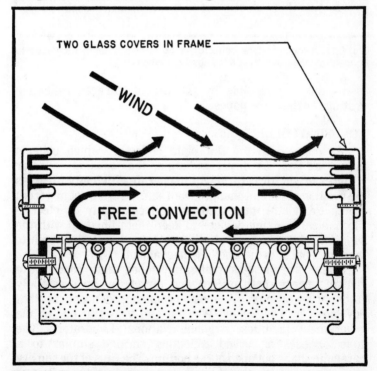

Fig. 3-10. Cross section of a solar collector showing air movement due to free and forced convection.

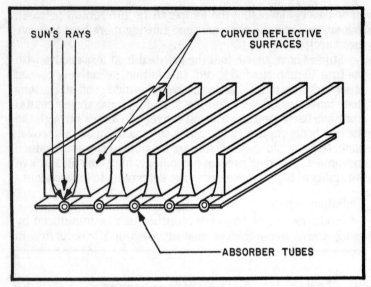

SUN'S RAYS

CURVED REFLECTIVE SURFACES

ABSORBER TUBES

Fig. 3-11. A focusing-type collector using curved reflective surfaces to concentrate the sun's rays on the absorber tubes.

losses may be possible by the use of infrared reflective coatings on the cover panes.

FOCUSING COLLECTORS

As opposed to the flat plate collector, which collects diffuse as well as direct radiation, the *focusing* collector requires bright, direct sunlight to operate efficiently. Also, as the position of the sun changes from sunrise to sunset and from month to month, most focusing collectors rely on electro-mechanical tracking devices to keep them lined up with the sun. Not only is this type of collector expensive and difficult to maintain, but so is the tracking mechanism.

There are designs being developed that concentrate radiant energy, both diffuse and direct, by an essentially stationary collector. A most promising concept is that developed by Dr. Roland Winston and tested at one of the government facilities, Argonne National Laboratory. The collector uses a curved reflecting surface similar to a parabolic shape but open at the bottom. The rays of the sun are concentrated on the absorber tubes at the base of the reflector. This concept is pictured in Fig. 3-11. One model being tested will heat liquid in the absorber tubes to 230°F—high enough for solar air conditioning, but too high and too expensive for practical home heating applications. This principle, however, may represent a breakthrough when solar energy is used to generate electricity, in addition to heating and cooling buildings. Additional research needs to be done, and it could be five to ten years before solar electricity is affordable.

The best place to use reflectors may be as reflective panels to direct additional energy on conventional flat plate collectors. The Towns School demonstration project described in Chapter 2 accomplished this, using aluminized Mylar as a reflective surface. The collectors were mounted in a *sawtooth* array, with the collector and reflector angled to complement each other (Fig. 3-12). Calculations predicted that the reflective surfaces, made of aluminized Mylar sheets bonded between clear Mylar and backed with ⅜ in. tempered

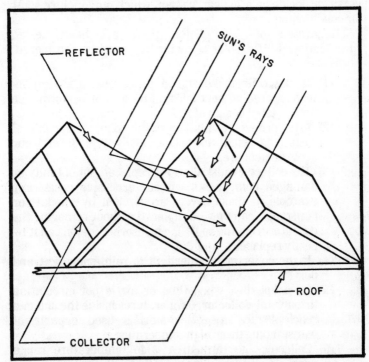

Fig. 3-12. The use of reflectors to increase radiation on flat-plate solar collectors.

hardboard, will increase solar radiation on the collectors by 30%. Alzak sheet, made by Alcoa, is also a good reflective material.

COLLECTOR REQUIREMENTS

I have discussed a variety of materials and design options that are available for the solar collector panel, and how efficiency can be improved by minimizing heat losses and using selective coatings and concentrating devices.

Generally speaking, the higher the efficiency, the lower the area of panels required to do the job. But you should not pay for collecting temperatures higher than what you actually need. You must determine what design represents the best potential value when used in a complete solar system for your home. This can vary depending on whether you want an inexpensive solar water heater, planning to replace it every 10 years, or decide on a 20-year system, which may include solar air conditioning.

Regardless of your choice, there are basic design specifications for the solar collector that must be considered. These are:

(1) Is the collector designed to be essentially maintenance-free without substantial loss of performance for its stated design life?

(2) After proper installation, is the collector capable of sustaining wind and snow loads typical of your geographical area?

(3) The collector must allow for replacement of faulty or damaged components without excessive costs. For example, if glass covers are broken by vandals or hailstones, can they be replaced without removing the collector from the roof? If an absorber leaks, can it be easily replaced?

(4) Is the collector weathertight to rain, snow, ice, and dust?

(5) On a hot day, when fluid or air is not circulating through the collector, temperatures inside the unit can reach 400°F. Are *all* materials used capable of withstanding these high temperatures?

(6) Collectors go through a wide temperature range during operation. Since different materials expand and contract in varying degrees, are adequate

provisions made to accommodate these dimensional changes?

(7) On liquid systems, the collector design must permit filling and draining of the working fluid easily. When a valve is opened, does gravity cause all the fluid to flow out of the collector, or does some remain trapped in the absorber coils?

(8) Are corrosion problems minimized through the proper selection of materials?

HEAT TRANSFER MEDIUM

Once heat is collected by the absorber, it must be transferred efficiently and economically to the storage tank. To do this, a *heat transfer medium* having a high thermal capacity and a low potential for corroding the absorber is required. At present, there are three basic choices: water, water plus organic liquids, and air. Each has particular advantages to offer, depending upon the overall system requirements. Before discussing the options, let's look at the properties of an *ideal* heat transfer fluid. The fluid must:

- Have a low viscosity (flows easily).
- Have a high heat capacity.
- Have a high fire point.
- Be noncorrosive to aluminum, copper, and steel.
- Be nonreactive to fluxes and cleaning compounds.
- Demand no fluid maintenance for at least ten years.
- Have a minimum pressure buildup.
- Cost below $5/gallon for every five years of service life.
- Be nonpoisonous.

Unfortunately, such an ideal fluid does not exist today, and you must make some compromises.

Tapwater

Straight tapwater is inexpensive, and compatible with copper plumbing. It can also be used for storage, eliminating the need for a heat exchanger. And it has a high heat capacity, so it will not burn, and is nonpoisonous. But there are some disadvantages to the use of untreated water. Water freezes at a relatively high temperature (32°F) and, to prevent damage, the collectors must be either drained or heated during freezing weather. (See Table 3-1, which gives the mean number of days

Table 3-1. Mean Number of Days Minimum Temperature 32°F and Below, Annually

ALABAMA			Colorado Springs	166
Birmingham	53		Denver	139
Mobile	18		Grand Junction	138
Montgomery	20		Pueblo	158
ALASKA			**CONNECTICUT**	
Anchorage	201		Bridgeport	101
Annette	79		Hartford	119
Barrow	323		New Haven	112
Barter Island	307		**DELAWARE**	
Bethel	225		Wilmington	102
Cold Bay	163		**DISTRICT OF COLUMBIA**	73
Cordova	191		**FLORIDA**	
Fairbanks	232		Apalachicola	4
Ft. Yukon	245		Daytona Beach	5
Juneau	146		Everglades	*
King Salmon	205		Ft. Myers	*
Kotzebue	252		Jacksonville	11
McGrath	231		Key West	0
Nome	241		Lakeland	1
St. Paul Island	189		Miami	*
Shemya	124		Miami Beach	0
Yakutat	171		Orlando	3
ARIZONA			Pensacola	9
Flagstaff	211		Tallahassee	20
Phoenix	17		Tampa	2
Prescott	131		West Palm Beach	*
Tucson	21		**GEORGIA**	
Winslow	132		Athens	49
Yuma	2		Atlanta	38
ARKANSAS			Augusta	54
Ft. Smith	71		Columbus	44
Little Rock	48		Macon	34
Texarkana	39		Rome	79
CALIFORNIA			Savannah	30
Bakersfield	15		Thomasville	14
Bishop	146		**HAWAII**	
Blue Canyon	102		Hilo	0
Burbank	4		Honolulu	0
Eureka	4		Lihue	0
Fresno	26		**IDAHO**	
Long Beach	1		Boise	128
Los Angeles	*		Idaho Falls	213
Mt. Shasta	135		Lewiston	101
Oakland	7		Pocatello	161
Red Bluff	23		**ILLINOIS**	
Sacramento	9		Cairo	64
Sandberg	54		Chicago	123
San Diego	*		Moline	139
San Francisco	6		Peoria	127
Santa Maria	15		Rockford	150
COLORADO			Springfield	121
Alamosa	226		**INDIANA**	

Table 3-1. (Continued)

Evansville	101	MISSISSIPPI	
Ft. Wayne	134	Jackson	36
Indianapolis	120	Meridian	47
South Bend	137	Vicksburg	21
IOWA		MISSOURI	
Burlington	128	Columbia	110
Des Moines	140	Kansas City	101
Dubuque	155	St. Joseph	127
Sioux City	152	St. Louis	83
Waterloo	158	Springfield	103
KANSAS		MONTANA	
Concordia	118	Billings	149
Dodge City	127	Butte	228
Goodland	156	Glasgow	184
Topeka	129	Great Falls	146
Wichita	112	Havre	172
KENTUCKY		Helena	182
Lexington	97	Kalispell	182
Louisville	92	Miles City	174
LOUISIANA		Missoula	181
Baton Rouge	18	NEBRASKA	
Lake Charles	12	Grand Island	150
New Orleans	4	Lincoln	129
Shreveport	31	Norfolk	158
MAINE		North Platte	178
Caribou	192	Omaha	136
Portland	160	Scottsbluff	180
MARYLAND		Valentine	164
Baltimore	71	NEVADA	
Frederick	119	Elko	214
MASSACHUSETTS		Ely	218
Blue Hill Obs.	132	Las Vegas	59
Boston	94	Reno	188
Nantucket	93	Winnemucca	195
Pittsfield	160	NEW HAMPSHIRE	
Worcester	148	Concord	168
MICHIGAN		Mt. Washington	242
Alpena	155	NEW JERSEY	
Detroit	125	Atlantic City	75
Escanaba	163	Newark	94
Flint	149	Trenton	89
Grand Rapids	150	NEW MEXICO	
Lansing	145	Albuquerque	107
Marquette	161	Clayton	144
Muskegon	144	Raton	185
Sault Ste. Marie	178	Roswell	99
MINNESOTA		NEW YORK	
Duluth	191	Albany	129
International Falls	199	Binghamton	134
Minneapolis	156	Buffalo	131
Rochester	166	New York	77
St. Cloud	178	Rochester	136

Table 3-1. (Continued)

Syracuse	135	Greenville	42
NORTH CAROLINA		Spartanburg	52
Asheville	83	**SOUTH DAKOTA**	
Cape Hatteras	13	Huron	169
Charlotte	65	Rapid City	158
Greensboro	85	Sioux Falls	169
Raleigh	73	**TENNESSEE**	
Wilmington	27	Bristol	94
Winston Salem	90	Chattanooga	51
NORTH DAKOTA		Knoxville	64
Bismarck	186	Memphis	57
Devils Lake	189	Nashville	74
Fargo	182	Oak Ridge	80
Williston	178	**TEXAS**	
OHIO		Abilene	45
Akron/Canton	136	Amarillo	111
Cincinnati	98	Austin	19
Cleveland	119	Brownsville	1
Columbus	117	Corpus Christi	5
Dayton	116	Dallas	33
Sandusky	111	El Paso	52
Toledo	121	Ft. Worth	32
Youngstown	136	Galveston	4
OKLAHOMA		Houston	7
Oklahoma City	70	Laredo	4
Tulsa	76	Lubbock	102
OREGON		Midland	64
Astoria	36	Port Arthur	11
Burns	184	San Angelo	42
Eugene	59	San Antonio	13
Meacham	170	Victoria	11
Medford	79	Waco	26
Pendleton	86	Wichita Falls	61
Portland	22	**UTAH**	
Roseburg	35	Milford	179
Salem	60	Salt Lake City	134
Sexton-Summit	112	Wendover	129
PENNSYLVANIA		**VERMONT**	
Allentown	129	Burlington	148
Erie	117	**VIRGINIA**	
Harrisburg	106	Lynchburg	78
Philadelphia	106	Norfolk	41
Pittsburgh	103	Richmond	71
Reading	92	Roanoke	86
Williamsport	130	**WASHINGTON**	
RHODE ISLAND		Olympia	84
Block Island	85	Seattle	20
Providence	106	Spokane	116
SOUTH CAROLINA		Stampede Pass	191
Charleston	33	Tatoosh Island	7
Columbia	31	Walla Walla	66
Florence	39	Yakima	130

Table 3-1. (Continued)

WEST VIRGINIA		WYOMING	
Charleston	97	Casper	174
Huntington	91	Cheyenne	174
Parkersburg	97	Lander	192
WISCONSIN		Sheridan	182
Green Bay	152	Yellowstone	210
La Crosse	153	PUERTO RICO	
Madison	143	San Juan	0
Milwaukee	129		

* less than once in 2 years

Climatic Atlas of the
United States,
U.S. Department of Commerce

when the temperature reaches 32° or lower for several cities across the country. The figures are accumulated on an annual basis.) Depending on your locality, the minerals in tapwater may cause deposits inside the absorber tubes and, over a period of time, cause a loss of efficiency. And tapwater cannot be used with aluminum without inhibitors or water treatment.

Organic Liquids

Organic liquids such as ethylene glycol have been used successfully with water in automobile radiators. Adding this chemical to the water serves to lower the freezing point and increase the boiling point of the mixture. For a 40% water, 60% glycol concentration (by weight), the freezing point of the mixture is below −50°F, the boiling point, 230°F at 1 atmosphere pressure. This is close to the maximum amount of ethylene glycol that can be mixed with water efficiently. With mixtures where the ethylene glycol approaches 70%, the freezing and boiling curves begin to reverse their directions. Thus a 30−70 solution will freeze at a higher temperature than will a 40−60 solution. Commercial antifreeze mixtures also contain corrosion inhibitors, another positive reason for using this mixture as a heat transfer fluid in the solar collector loop.

There are also some disadvantages to consider, however. For example, adding ethylene glycol to water reduces its specific heat. This means that the resulting mixture will not store the same energy in a given volume that water alone will. At 160°F the 40–60 mixture stores only 80% as much as straight water. For this reason (plus cost) it is not practical to use a glycol mixture in the storage tank. If it is selected for the collector loop, a heat exchanger must be employed. Over the normal operating temperature range of the collector, the volume of a 40–60 solution will increase 9%, and an expansion tank in the collector loop is necessary.

Commercial antifreeze mixtures decay over a period of time, producing acidic concentrations. These acids are harmful to metal and, therefore, if used in the collector loop, periodic draining and replacement of the fluid is necessary, just as is required in an automobile radiator. There are several brands of commercial antifreeze; if aluminum absorbers are used, be sure the antifreeze is the same as that used with aluminum-block automobile engines.

There are at least a dozen other organic fluids manufactured by leading companies, such as Dow-Corning, Dow Chemical, General Electric, and Monsanto, that are suitable heat transfer fluids for solar systems. Most of them have been used in industrial and commercial applications with a good performance record, and each may offer a specific advantage for a given system. The specific choice is best left to the system designer. Just one word of caution: Don't use alcohol, because it poses both fire and health hazards. At high temperatures alcohol tends to boil out of a solution, forming a concentrated vapor that is potentially explosive and possibly toxic.

Air

The use of air as a transfer medium seems like a logical choice if the only purpose of the solar system is to heat the air inside the house. With this objective, some expensive heat exchangers may be eliminated. Air is free, noncorrosive, and will not freeze, and minor system leaks do not cause severe problems. Unfortunately, there are also disadvantages to its use. Air requires larger pumps, and more electrical energy to run them. Higher airflow rates cause noisier systems, and the ductwork takes up a substantial amount of space. An air system is not as flexible as a liquid system for water heating applications, and I know of no way to utilize air collectors for cost-effective solar air conditioning.

HEAT STORAGE MATERIALS

At present, there are three choices for *heat storage* material: water, rock, or eutectic salts. Of these three, water is the most common choice. It is inexpensive and has a high heat-storing capacity. Next is rock, which heats slowly but retains heat longer than water. Eutectic salts, such as Glauber's salt, have a low melting point and store heat when they melt. The use of these salts as a heat storage material is promising; but they are still in the experimental stage, and have yet to prove their reliability. Consequently, they should not be considered for use in a solar heating system at this time. One of the big problems that plague these salts is their loss of effectiveness after frequent changes between the solid and liquid states. Paraffin waxes are also candidate storage materials but, like the salts, further research is required before they can be recommended.

Engineers use what they call the *specific heat principle* to compare storage materials. Specific heat (C) is a measure of the amount of heat energy a material can hold for every degree its temperature is raised. Water has a specific heat of 1.0, rock, 0.21. The units for specific heat are Btu per pound of mass per degree of temperature (Btu/1bm-°F). To calculate the amount of heat energy a given material can hold, its specific heat is multiplied by its density in pounds of mass per cubic foot (1bm/ft^3). In comparing the heat capacity (C) for water

$$C = 1 \text{ (Btu/1bm-°F)} \times 62.4 \text{ (1bm/ft}^3\text{)}$$
$$= 62.4 \text{ Btu/ft}^3\text{-°F}$$

and, for crushed rock

$$C = 0.21 \text{ (Btu/1bm-°F)} \times 100 \text{ (1bm/ft}^3\text{)}$$
$$= 21 \text{ Btu/ft}^3$$

These calculations tell us that water will hold approximately three times the heat that rock will hold for the same amount of storage space.

There will continue to be arguments, pro and con, between manufacturers about which is the better storage material, water or rock. It is my opinion, however, that water is the better choice for systems using water as a heat transfer medium, and rock is the best selection for an air system.

STORAGE TANKS

Several *storage tank* materials have been tried in federally funded, solar energy demonstration projects and by do-it-yourself experimenters. Among the more common materials are:

- Standard-building water tanks made from galvanized steel.
- Steel fuel-oil storage tanks.
- Concrete septic tanks.
- Fiberglass.
- Galvanized-steel drain culvert.
- Concrete building pipe.

As with other parts of the system, the storage tank should require minimum maintenance over its design life. If the tank is to hold water, leakage and corrosion must be minimized, and the tank material must withstand the operating pressure and temperature of the stored water.

Selecting a Storage Tank

Cylindrical tanks made of galvanized steel are the most popular choice, due to price and availability. If you do not plan to store potable (drinkable) water, a less expensive fuel-oil tank is worth considering. These tanks are not high-pressure containers and, if used, a vent allowing for pressure built-up from boiling must be provided. Venting also requires a provision for adding cold *makeup* water due to losses. A small amount of some rust preventive should be added to the stored water, and other corrosion-preventive measures should be adopted. When using metal tanks, keep in mind that different metals must be electrically isolated to prevent electrolytic corrosion of the tank. Copper plumbing lines connected directly to a steel tank would cause a corrosion problem. A dielectric (nonconducting) fitting or neoprene hose may be used to separate different metals.

If you are considering precast concrete storage for systems other than rock storage, using air as a transfer medium, you should be aware that leaks have been a problem on several projects. Expansion, contraction, and settling, in addition to porosity, requires sealing. Butyl rubber works better than epoxy for this purpose. Regardless of the material selected, if you plan to store potable water, be sure that the

tank or liner will not contaminate it. After reviewing the specifications, check with your local building inspector.

Minimizing Heat Losses

For efficient operation, heat losses from storage tanks must be minimized. You would not want to lose more than 10% of the collected heat, even on the coldest nights; design with a maximum loss of 5% would be a better choice.

The loss depends upon the properties and thickness of the particular insulation chosen, as well as the physical location of the storage tank. An ideal location would be under a portion of the house to be heated. Here, heat lost would still make a positive contribution, except in summer months when heat is not desirable. For existing homes, the usual choice is the basement. For new homes, burying the storage tank beneath the basement or ground floor is a popular option. With the exception of rock storage, which does not lose heat as rapidly, aboveground storage outside the heated structure is not recommended. Although determining the size of the storage tank will be discussed in more detail in Chapter 5, we are basically talking about short-term storage; for example, a tank that would provide heat during two sunless days.

HEAT EXCHANGERS

Whenever it is necessary to transfer heat from one liquid to another without mixing them, or to transfer heat from liquid to air or vice versa, a *heat exchanger* is used. For example, Fig. 2-3 shows a liquid heat exchanger in operation. An antifreeze/water solution is used in the solar collector *loop* to prevent freezing. It is not practical to fill a storage tank with it, however, due to the expense, so plain water is used in the tank.

These liquids are separated by using an exchanger of the type shown in Fig. 3-13. The hot antifreeze mixture from the collectors flows through the continuous metal coil, heating adjacent water. This particular exchanger, called the *shell and tube* type, has a copper coil and steel casing, although other metals may be used. Note that the collector fluid flows in an opposite direction to the storage water. Called a single-pass counterflow design, this keeps the temperature difference between fluids nearly constant along the length of the exchanger. The result is more efficient heat transfer. The same type of exchanger may also be used where it is

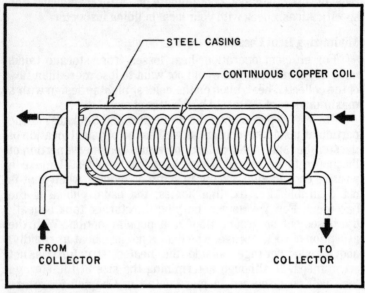

Fig. 3-13. A device used to exchange heat between two liquids. This particular exchanger is a shell and tube type, using a copper coil and a steel casing.

necessary to prevent contamination of drinkable water, as in a solar water heater.

The liquid-to-air heat exchange unit is a part of both the room heating system (Fig. 2-5) and the solar air conditioner (Fig. 2-6). As the drawings indicate, these units are located in the furnace chamber.

Figure 3-14 shows the construction of a typical liquid-to-air exchanger. For heating, the blower fan forces air past the exchanger that has hot water circulating through the tubes. The air, warmed by convection and radiation, is circulated by the fan through the heating ducts to the rooms. Conversely, for the air-conditioning cycle, chilled refrigerant flows through the tubes of the exchanger, and the rooms are cooled.

COLLECTOR FILTER

The heat transfer fluid used in a collector loop should have continuous *filtration*. This is especially important in systems using aluminum absorbers. Severe pitting due to galvanic corrosion can occur if small particles of dissimilar metals are carried by the fluid into the collectors and become trapped.

This is quite possible with absorbers of the "sandwich" type, which can have a very restrictive flow path. Although the filter will cause a pressure drop, this can be minimized by using a filter cartridge that is relatively coarse. One that filters particles of 350 microns in size (0.0138 in. *or* 0.35 mm) will do an adequate job.

GETTER

The word *getter* may sound strange to you just as it did to me. Actually, it's a term used to describe one of the simplest components in the system. As a companion to the collector filter, this device is installed in the collector-piping loop just before the fluid enters the filter. It is needed with aluminum absorbers to react with copper or iron ions that may be

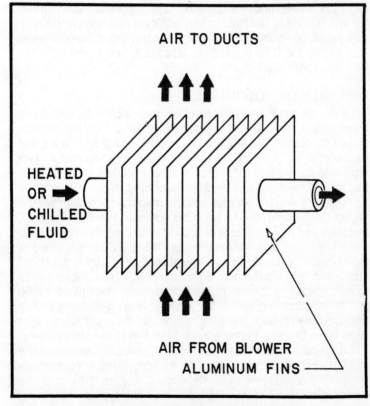

Fig. 3-14. A typical liquid-to-air heat exchanger.

dissolved in the circulating fluid. A suggested design is a coil of aluminum window screen placed inside a 2 in. diameter radiator-type rubber hose. The copper ions corrode the fine screen wire, rather than the expensive collector absorbers. The filter will trap any small particles of the aluminum screen that may break off and enter the fluid stream.

EXPANSION TANK

An *expansion* or *surge* tank is recommended for installation on the outlet side of the collector. In the discussion on the heat transfer medium, it was pointed out that a 40% water, 60% ethylene glycol solution will expand in volume by 9% over the typical operating range of the collector. In addition, a pump failure causing a lack of circulation on a hot day may cause further expansion. The expansion tank allows for any boiling of the fluid in the collector or pressure buildup that could be caused by a power failure. The expansion tank also allows for fluid expansion, and yet it keeps the collector loop filled with fluid.

DIFFERENTIAL THERMOSTAT

Just as your present furnace and water heater have thermostats to control temperature, a solar heating system should be similarly equipped. The major difference in a solar thermostat is that it must measure and compare two temperatures rather than one. A device called a *differential thermostat* has been designed for solar operation.

One of the more popular units is manufactured by the Rho Sigma Company in California. This unit uses two heat sensors, one attached to the surface of a solar-collector absorber plate, the other at the water storage tank. When the temperature of the collector exceeds that of the stored water by a specified amount, a relay in the unit closes, starting the collector pump motor. The pump circulates the fluid through the collector loop of the system. (Figure 2-4 shows this plumbing.) The thermostat prevents pumping action on overcast days or at night when the heat in storage would be lost to the atmosphere.

A good differential thermostat prevents unnecessary on-off "cycling" of the pump by incorporating a reasonable temperature differential in its circuit. Figure 3-15, and the explanation that follows, will describe the typical operating cycle for one day's operation.

The collector pump is initially *off*. As the sun rises at 7:00 a.m., the collector temperature increases rapidly above the storage tank temperature. At point 1, which is 20°F above the tank temperature, the thermostat relay closes, starting the pump motor. As the cooler fluid in the tank begins to circulate, it causes an initial drop in the collector temperature, to point 2. As long as the collector temperature remains 3°F or more above the tank temperature, the pump continues to operate. As evening approaches, the collector temperature falls. When it is less than 3°F above the tank temperature, at point 3, the pump is turned off. Once fluid flow stops, there is a temporary rise in temperature, to point 4. As long as the temperature at this point is less than 20°F above the temperature of the tank, the pump remains off until sunrise. This differential-thermostat control system, with factory settings, assures that maximum heat energy is stored and retained in the tank under various weather conditions.

Some units locate the solar collector sensor in the waterline, where the water leaves the last collector, rather than attaching it to the absorber plate. I personally prefer this approach for liquid systems, as it directly measures the temperature of the water leaving the collector. Figures 3-16 and 3-17 show a Rho Sigma sensor and recommended installation. For systems using airflow, rather than a liquid flow, attaching the sensor directly to the absorber is

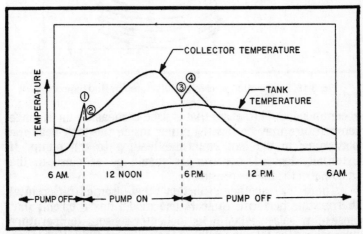

Fig. 3-15. Daily operating cycle of a circulating pump controlled by a differential thermostat.

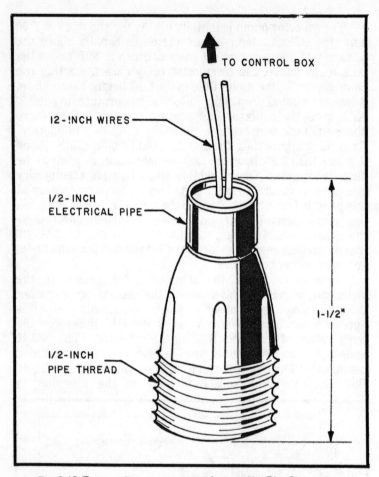

Fig. 3-16. Temperature sensor, manufactured by Rho Sigma, Inc.

recommended. The sensor that is used to measure the storage temperature may be located either inside the tank near the bottom or in the exit waterline leading to the pump. If externally located, however, it should be as close to the tank-end of the line as possible.

There is another function that some differential thermostats perform. At least one model has a circuit that closes a relay when the collector-sensor temperature approaches the freezing point of the collector fluid. If you live in an area where freezing temperatures occur and an

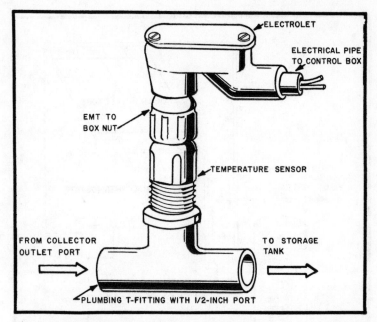

Fig. 3-17. Recommended method of installing the solar temperature sensor for a liquid system.

antifreeze solution is not used in the collector fluid, this feature can prevent collector damage due to freezing. There are two typical functions that may be controlled by this relay: opening valves to drain the collector; and activating electrical heating elements installed in the collector to warm them above the freezing point. A typical connection of a differential thermostat is shown in Fig. 3-18.

VARIABLE FLOW CONTROL

Another control that may or may not be incorporated into the differential thermostat assembly is a *variable flow* controller. This device controls the speed of the circulating pump in the collector loop as a function of the absorber temperature. For example, a slow flow of liquid through the absorber results in higher outlet temperatures than does a fast flow. There is an optimum balance to achieve, since the collector efficiency decreases as the absorber temperature increases (due to heat losses). Varying the flow rate helps improve the overall efficiency of the system.

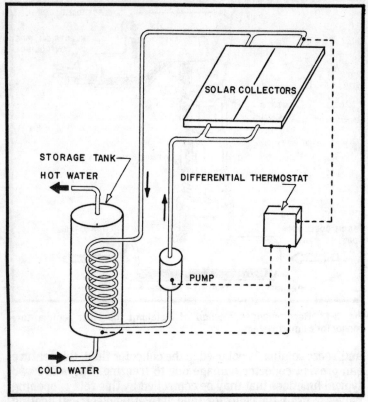

Fig. 3-18. A typical method of connecting a differential thermostat.

The Rho Sigma model 142 proportional (variable flow) controller has been designed to operate with the Grundfos UPS 20-42 model pump. Figure 3-19 shows an operating profile of this pump with too high a flow rate for the given *insolation* (solar heating) level. Three curves are plotted for insolation levels of 100, 200, and 300 Btu/ft^2-hr. These curves were plotted for a typical double-glazed collector with a flat-black absorber. Mathematical derivations are published in Rho Sigma's *Solar Energy Engineering and Product Catalog*. Delta T (ΔT) is the difference between the absorber temperature and the storage tank. Along the bottom axis is the fluid flow rate in gallons per minute divided by the collector area in square feet.

For example, 50 sq ft of collector panels with a flow rate of 5 gallons per minute would have a fluid flow rate of 5/50 = 0.1, as defined on the curve. As expected, as the flow rate increases, the ΔT decreases. Initially, at point 1 ($\Delta T = 0$), the pump is *off*. As the collector absorber warms and reaches 20°F above the storage temperature, at point 2, the pump is turned *on*. Assume the insolation level at this time is 200 Btu/ft^2-hr, and the flow rate of the pump has been set at 0.1 gallons per minute per square foot of collector area. Once fluid flow starts, the absorber is cooled, following a path down the 200 curve. Once it reaches point 3 ($\Delta T = 3°F$), the pump is turned off; the flow goes back to zero (point 4) and the absorber temperature climbs again toward point 2.

This *cycling* of the pump and the unstable operation will continue until the insolation level climbs to 300 Btu/ft^2-hr and

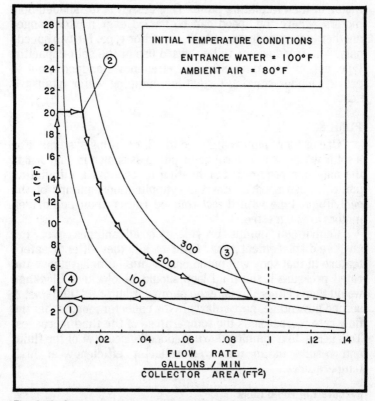

Fig. 3-19. Operating profile of the Rho Sigma variable flow control. The curves were plotted for a typical double-glazed collector with a flat-black absorber.

the flow rate of 0.1 gallon per minute can be sustained. If you could vary the rate of flow, setting it, for instance, at 0.075 when the insolation level was 200, then increasing it to 0.1 when the insolation level increased to 300, not only would continuous operation result, but you would achieve greater efficiency by keeping the ΔT from becoming excessive. (In Chapter 5, Fig. 5-4 plots typical collector efficiencies as a function of ΔT.)

The proportional controller activates a switch on the Grundfos pump motor, changing its speed from 1900 rpm (revolutions per minute) to 2620 rpm at the correct insolation level. All of these operations could presumably be performed manually, but it would require almost constant monitoring, and not many homeowners would want this chore.

Be sure you choose the correct control for the type of motor in the circulating pump. One design is for shaded-pole motors, where the speed can be varied over a wide range; another is for a permanent split-capacitor type, for two speeds only. The trend seems to be toward use of the split-capacitor type, not only from an electrical efficiency standpoint, but to provide higher starting torque for pumping water against a head.

PUMPS

One or more *pumps* are used in solar heating systems. For a solar water heater, a collector pump as shown in Fig. 3-18 is the only one required. For heating or cooling, a circulating pump is also needed. For these applications, pumps of the centrifugal type with direct-coupled rather than belt-driven motors are suggested.

Centrifugal pumps provide two advantages over the positive-displacement type. First of all, they offer a safety feature in that they will pump only a small amount above the rated pressure if the fluid loop should be blocked. Blockage would then neither damage the pump nor burst its fluid line. A second advantage, particularly in the collector loop, is that the flow rate increases as the temperature of the fluid increases. This is due to a thinning down (reduced viscosity) of the fluid, and results in an improved collector efficiency at high temperatures.

Calculating Head Loss

The pumps selected by the system manufacturer should provide for the proper specific pressure (*head*) versus flow rate requirements. In reviewing manufacturers' literature, you will see that pump ratings plot the total *head* of water in feet against the capacity or flow rate in gallons per minute. Collector manufacturers should provide a recommended flow rate and head loss for their respective units. Let's assume that a l gpm (gallon per minute) flow rate through each collector is suggested, and the collectors are connected in parallel as in Fig. 3-20. If five collectors are used, the pump must have a flow rate capability of 5 gpm. But if the collectors are in series, as in Fig. 3-21, to get a flow rate of 1 gpm through each collector requires a pump capability of approximately 1 gpm.

To calculate head losses, the system manufacturer should add the effect of all components in the collector loop to get a total loss. This includes line loss and pressure drops across the filter, getter, heat exchanger, valves, collectors, and any other components that would impede the flow of the collector fluid. Normally, small pumps of 1/12 or even 1/20 of a horsepower will provide the recommended flow rates in the collector loop if the loop is *closed* and remains full of fluid. The pump then must only circulate the fluid, and not pump it vertically from the storage tank to the collectors.

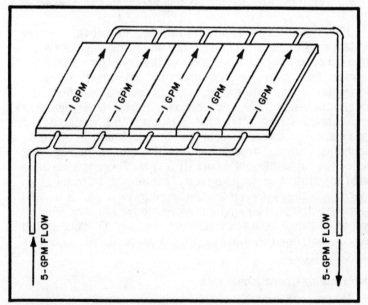

Fig. 3-20. The flow rate through five collectors connected in parallel.

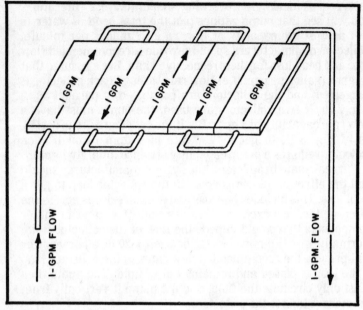

Fig. 3-21. The flow rate through five collectors connected in series.

If the collectors are self-draining, to provide freeze protection, the pump must have the total head capacity at *no flow* equal to the height (in feet) of the collectors above the storage tank *plus* an allowance for frictional losses in horizontal lines, fittings, and filters before reaching the maximum height. This, of course, is a much greater pumping requirement. In the latter case, a pump with a variable flow rate control is a good investment. One such unit is made by Grundfos Pumps Corporation, and the curves in Fig. 3-22 define the capabilities of model UPS 20-42. There is a variable head adjustment on the pump body that allows you to select an operating range between the dashed curves A and B at 1900 rpm. A switch on the pump increases the rpm to 2620, with an operating range between solid curves C and D. This switch may be activated by the Rho Sigma proportional controller just described.

Determining Operational Costs

Pumps and controls are the only components in a solar system that use electrical energy; to obtain the maximum number of Btu per dollar of solar system cost, the operating cost of the pump(s) should be taken into consideration. It is incorrect to assume that pump flow is always evenly proportional to the horsepower (hp) rating. Different pump designs have different efficiencies.

Most consumers do not have the expertise necessary to evaluate pump efficiency, but there is a simple way to check on pump selection. First, the head requirements of the system must be known. If the salesman doesn't know, have him get the answer for you (and put it in writing). Second, obtain the performance curves (Fig. 3-22) for different units of several

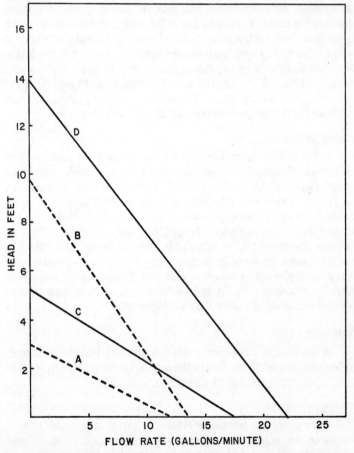

Fig. 3-22. A performance curve for the Grundfos pump, model UPS 20-42.

manufacturers, including the one in the system under consideration. Determine the flow rate in gallons per minute provided by each pump, operating at the particular head your system requires. Third, divide the gallons per minute provided by each pump by its specific horsepower rating. The pump yielding the greatest number, as a result of this calculation, will be the least expensive to operate electrically if the manufacturer's literature is correct. Warranty, repair, maintenance, noise, and vibration are other factors to consider in pump selection.

I explained the need for a greater pumping capacity on self-draining systems over closed loop systems circulating antifreeze. Just what does this greater pump capacity cost to operate? A calculation was made for a system operating at a 5 gpm flow rate, with a head of 25 ft for the self-draining concept and 7 ft for the closed loop. At an electricity cost of 3¢ per k Wh, the operating cost of the circulation pump in each system was found to be $12.47/yr for the self-draining system and $5.40/yr for the closed loop system. This difference is not great, but it is another factor for you to consider in system selection.

Pump Materials

I would like to make one last comment on pumps. The selection of materials from which a pump is made should be carefully regarded. In closed loop systems circulating inhibited water or ethylene glycol, a cast iron pump is satisfactory and less expensive. When the system is open to the atmosphere, or intended for potable use, stainless steel or bronze are essential to eliminate rust buildup, and often to comply with local plumbing codes. Local code restrictions vary throughout the country, and you should check with your specific municipality. It is my opinion that cast iron pumps should not be used to circulate drinking water.

VALVES

A discussion on *valves* is often neglected, but the improper selection, installation, or placement of these units can lead to malfunctions or excessive maintenance costs.

Value Operation

An *automatic pressure relief* valve of adequate size is required for any system containing pressurized fluids. These valves should be set to open at not less than 25% in excess of the working pressure, and not more than the maximum pressure for which the system is designed. Figure 3-23 shows a standard pressure-only relief valve for use with water heaters equipped with energy cutoffs. This unit has a test lever for manual operation. In some cases, both temperature and pressure are regulated in one unit, and these have an extension-type thermal element available in different lengths to place the temperature sensing element in the hottest zone. A typical temperature/pressure valve is pictured in Fig. 3-24.

By design, all *temperature/pressure relief* valves are intended to protect a water heater or storage tank from dangerous overtemperature or excessive pressure. The valves accomplish this by opening to discharge the stored liquid. A small amount may be discharged due to thermal expansion of the fluid, a large amount if the valve opens because the temperature is excessive. A drain pipe should be provided to prevent injury from discharges and to carry away ejected

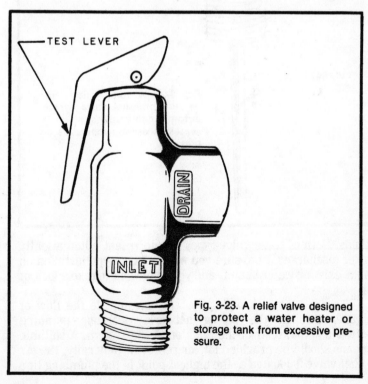

Fig. 3-23. A relief valve designed to protect a water heater or storage tank from excessive pressure.

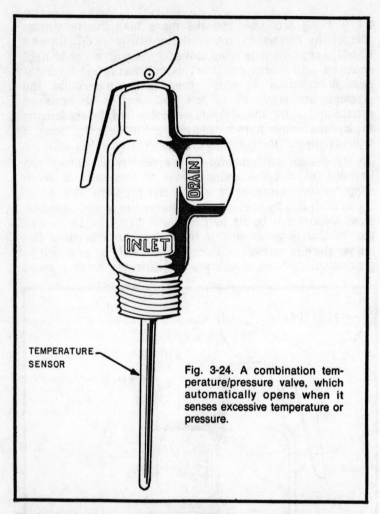

TEMPERATURE
SENSOR

Fig. 3-24. A combination temperature/pressure valve, which automatically opens when it senses excessive temperature or pressure.

fluids. Both of these valve-types should reseat automatically after discharges. I am sure you will find one type installed on your existing water heater, and you may want to take a look at it.

Trapped air in a piping system can impede the flow of liquids through the piping network, decrease pumping efficiency, and restrict the function of the system. A suitable means should be provided for air removal. Generally, the *air relief* valve is located at the highest point in the plumbing line of the collector loop. This valve may also function to allow air back into the line to facilitate draining water from the collector loop, providing freeze protection for those systems not relying on antifreeze.

Types of Valves

Valves to prevent the backflow of fluids are commonly called *check valves*. As their name implies, they allow fluid to flow in one direction only. A valve of this type is suggested on solar water-heating systems. In Chapter 4, Fig. 4-8 shows a typical placement of the check valve (V-3) in the system.

Another valve that is frequently recommended on solar water heaters is a *tempering* valve. Under optimum conditions, 180°F water can be collected. To prevent the possibility of scalding, a tempering valve is installed (see Fig. 3-25) which automatically mixes hot and cold water to the

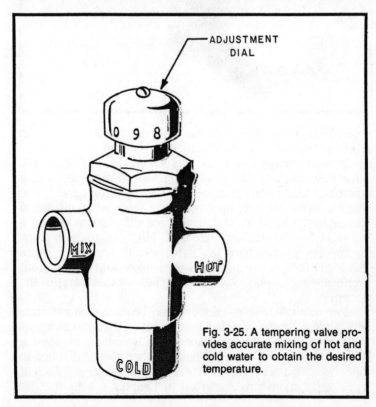

Fig. 3-25. A tempering valve provides accurate mixing of hot and cold water to obtain the desired temperature.

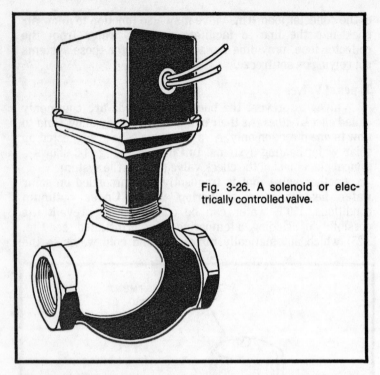

Fig. 3-26. A solenoid or electrically controlled valve.

desired maximum temperature. The valve pictured has an adjustment dial to vary the thermostatic control.

In more complex systems, this job can also be done by a three-way *solenoid* valve. Solenoid valves are electrically operated, using the principle of an electromagnet. The solenoid-valve coil sets up a magnetic force when electrical current is flowing through it. This force either opens or closes the valve port, controlling fluid flow. Most designs also allow for manual operation of the valve when necessary. These valves are designed to operate using independent signals from thermostats, relays, motors, or switches in other parts of the system.

For example, a solenoid valve may be energized and open only while a pump motor is running, automatically closing as the motor stops. Another application would be to open a solenoid drain valve if an independent thermostat attached to the solar collectors "sensed" freezing temperatures. (Both of these applications are described in Chapter 4 with specific reference to Fig. 4-8.) These valves are easily identified by the electrical wires coming out of them. Their appearance is typical of that pictured in Fig. 3-26. Like other precision valves, they are manufactured to close tolerances, and care must be taken to prevent dirt, scale, or sludge from jamming the valve. The use of a filter upstream from the valve is recommended.

SOLAR COLLECTOR LOOP

The complete *solar collector loop*, with all components installed, is shown in Fig. 3-27. As you will see in the following chapter on typical system arrangements, all of these components may not always be required. A case in point is a solar water heater using copper plumbing and absorber plates.

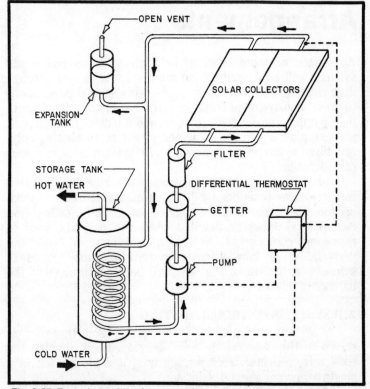

Fig. 3-27. Typical plumbing for a complete solar collector loop, with a getter for the aluminum absorbers and a differential thermostat for control.

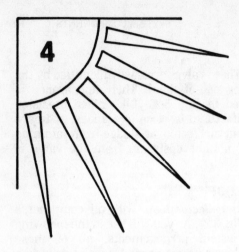

Typical System Arrangements

For space or room heating, both air systems and liquid systems will be described. An air system with rock storage does not require a heat exchanger or any special precautions to prevent corrosion or freezing; but it has the disadvantage of high pumping-power requirements and a lack of flexibility. If you are planning to use solar energy for room heating only, and have a forced-air heater, an air system is worth your consideration.

Adaptations of systems previously described will be used in various combinations by different manufacturers. In most product literature, standard engineering symbols, rather than isometric sketches or detailed cross sections, are used to represent components. Now that you have a basic understanding of how a solar system operates, standard symbols, as shown in Fig. 4-1, will be used throughout the balance of this book.

AIR SYSTEMS FOR ROOM HEATING

A system designed by International Solarthermics is shown in Fig. 4-2. This is a self-contained unit, having the collectors, reflector, rock-storage unit, and blower fan in a single triangular-shaped container.

This unit is designed to be mounted in the yard at ground level. It should be located as close to the house as possible to

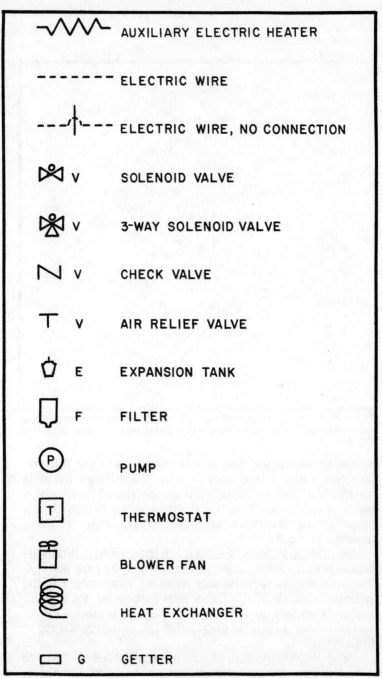

-\/\/\/-		AUXILIARY ELECTRIC HEATER
--------		ELECTRIC WIRE
--|--		ELECTRIC WIRE, NO CONNECTION
▷◁	V	SOLENOID VALVE
▷◁	V	3-WAY SOLENOID VALVE
N	V	CHECK VALVE
T	V	AIR RELIEF VALVE
▽	E	EXPANSION TANK
▽	F	FILTER
P		PUMP
T		THERMOSTAT
▯		BLOWER FAN
◎		HEAT EXCHANGER
▭	G	GETTER

Fig. 4-1. Symbols used in schematic drawings of solar energy systems.

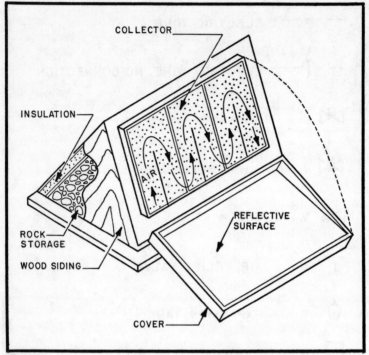

Fig. 4-2. An air collector and storage unit designed by International Solarthermics. The collector uses a cup arrangement, similar to that in Fig. 3-5.

minimize heat losses. The rock is stored inside the A-frame structure, filling it from floor to peak. The collector fan pulls air into the solar collector, through the stored rocks and a series of baffles and heat traps. Here, the air is heated as it passes through a series of aluminum cups in staggered rows, as shown in Fig. 3-5.

As in other systems, a differential thermostat is used. One sensor is in the solar collector, the other in the rock storage. The collector fan operates only when the temperature in the collector exceeds that of the stored rock by an amount sufficient enough to increase the storage temperature. A second blower, called the distribution fan, is also contained in the A-frame.

When the thermostat on your present forced-air furnace calls for heat, the distribution fan on the solar furnace is turned on, forcing air through the heated rock and into the plenum of your present furnace. Cold air is drawn from your home back into the storage area to be reheated. If the heat stored in the rock falls below that required for the house, the conventional forced-air furnace must carry the heating load until the heat of the sun is sufficient to increase the temperature of the stored rock to approximately 75°F.

This unit also uses a reflector to improve efficiency. The reflective surface is on the inside surface of a hinged cover, which is closed during the summertime when heat is not required. Many of these units have been sold; but as with any system you may be considering, try to talk with several owners who have used them throughout the winter season to get first-hand reports on performance.

FUNCTION OF LIQUID SYSTEMS

For room heating using a liquid transfer medium, the system shown in Fig. 4-3 is suggested. Notice that the solar collector piping is a conventional closed loop, circulating an antifreeze mixture. The operation of the solar heater is

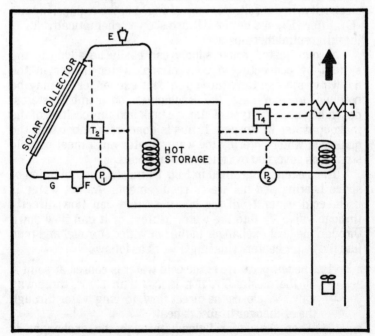

Fig. 4-3. Solar room heating using a closed loop liquid system.

controlled by your house thermostat (T_4). Let's say, for example, that it is set at 72°F and the inside air temperature falls below this point. Room heat will be supplied in one of two ways:

- If the temperature of the solar-heated water in storage exceeds 85°F, distribution pump P_2 starts. Hot water from storage is circulated through the coils of a heat exchanger, located above the blower fan. The coils radiate heat, which is distributed through the house by the blower and duct network.

- With a storage temperature below 85°F, an auxiliary electric heating element, located in the distribution duct, supplies room heat. No pumping occurs, for at low storage temperatures you could spend more money on electricity to operate the pump than could be saved in fuel costs.

As solar energy will be more cost-effective in homes that presently have electric room- and water-heaters, the auxiliary heater shown in this and other examples will be powered by electricity. In the collector loop of Fig. 4-3, the expansion tank (E), filter (F), and getter (G) are shown schematically. T_2 is the differential thermostat.

A solar-heated water supply can easily be added to the system by connecting a conventional water heater in the hot-water storage tank through a heat exchanger. It may be possible to eliminate the exchanger on some systems, depending upon the type of storage tank and composition of the makeup water in storage. If this is done, remember that the quality of water entering the water heater must meet potable standards governed by strict building codes.

The system diagramed in Fig. 4-4 meets a combination of space heating and hot water requirements. As hot water is used, cold water from the house system can flow directly through valve V_1 into the water heater; or it can flow down through the heat exchanger in the hot water storage, and then into the water heater. This might work as follows.

1) The temperature of the cold water is sensed at point A by thermostat T_1. If it is less than 150°F, three-way valve V_1 closes the direct flow, forcing water through the exchanger to absorb heat.

2) When the water flowing through the exchanger is heated to a temperature in excess of 150°F, the sensor

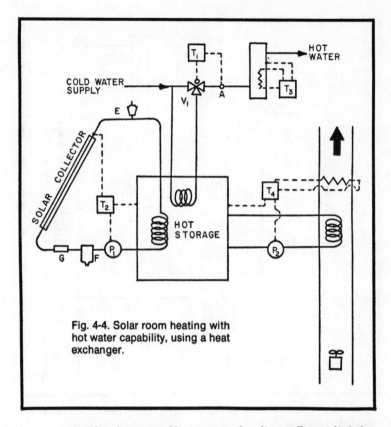

COLD WATER SUPPLY

HOT WATER

SOLAR COLLECTOR

HOT STORAGE

Fig. 4-4. Solar room heating with hot water capability, using a heat exchanger.

at point A causes V_1 to open the direct flow, slightly mixing hot and cold water in correct proportions.

3) Water, from either source, then flows into the water heater. If the solar-heated water is insufficient to maintain a temperature of 140°F in the water heater, thermostat T_3 activates the electric resistance coil in the unit, boosting the temperature.

As freeze protection is provided in the collector loop, no drain-down is necessary. The added cost of the heat exchanger, getter, and expansion tank is partially offset by using a less expensive aluminum absorber in the collector, rather than a copper absorber. Also, as you will observe throughout this chapter, a closed loop system provides flexibility for a total hot water, room heat, and air-conditioning package.

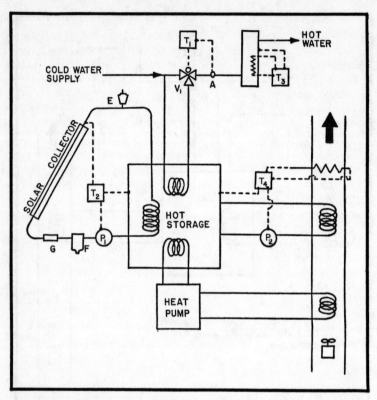

Fig. 4-5. A combined system for room heating, water heating, and a solar-assisted heat pump.

Now we come to the beauty of a hot-water storage system—its flexibility. By adding a heat pump to the system (Fig. 4-5), you can have solar-assisted room heating *plus* hot water from central storage. In addition, the heat pump will air-condition the house, but it does so without any contribution from the solar system. A heat pump is basically an air conditioner with reversing valves. When fluid flows in one direction, heat is produced; when it flows in the opposite direction, heat is absorbed, resulting in air conditioning.

HEAT PUMPS

A heat pump operates on electricity like a conventional vapor-compression type home air conditioner, with one major exception—it can heat, as well as cool, by reversing the cycle.

A refrigerator, for example, is a simple heat pump. For heating purposes, this unit gets much more out of a dollar's worth of electricity than electric resistance elements used in baseboard heaters or electric furnaces. Moreover, it delivers the same amount of heat using approximately one-fourth as much electricity.

As with air conditioners, a portion of the heat pump is exposed to the outdoors. When the heat pump is operating as an air conditioner, it absorbs heat inside the house and rejects it outdoors. Keep in mind that it does this operating on conventional electric power, with no help from the solar system. For the heating mode, its operation is reversed. The pump absorbs low-grade energy from the outside air, warms it to the desired temperature, and circulates it inside the house. Here, solar energy can assist the heat pump, providing higher temperatures from water storage than are available from the outdoors. This increases the efficiency of the heat pump and lowers the amount of electrical energy it uses.

Most heat pumps will not be effective if outdoor temperatures are below 30°F. In this case, without solar storage, the electric resistance heater in the pump package would provide all of the heating at a very high cost. On the coldest days in winter, which tend to be clear, the solar collectors operate at their best efficiency, the heat pump at its lowest. Together, as a solar-assisted heat pump, these devices combine into a most efficient heating system. Both units can then be smaller in size than if used individually, resulting in cost savings. Although individual system designs may vary, a typical system might function as follows.

- If the water in the storage tank is at a temperature of 104°F or greater, it is circulated directly through the heat exchanger in the distribution duct, bypassing the heat pump.
- If the stored water is at a temperature between 40°F and 103°F, and above the outdoor temperature, the stored water becomes the heat pump.
- If the outdoor temperature is above that of the stored water, it then becomes the heat source for the heat pump.
- If the heat pump is operating, and it is unable to meet the room temperature called for by the thermostat, an auxiliary electric-resistance heating element is turned on automatically.

You will hear a lot of positive publicity about solar-assisted heat pumps, since many electric utilities feel that this approach is to their advantage. As you might suspect, widespread use of solar energy would decrease power consumption; but the solar-assisted heat pump provides a very workable compromise. Solar energy would reduce the level of peak power consumption during the daylight hours, while the heat pumps would still require electricity at night. Thus, the promotion of the solar-assisted heat pump concept insures not only a future market for the electric utilities, but a means of smoothing out power fluctuations.

Heat pumps are more reliable today than they were back in the 1950s and early 1960s, when they were vigorously sold to a disappointed public. The unreliability of the compressors in those earlier units, coupled with poor installation and service, caused most of the complaints. This is not to say that further design improvements are unwarranted. Small-size heat pumps for residential applications generally use single compressors, which limit the efficient operating range of the unit. The development of heat pump systems that are specifically designed for operating efficiently both at low outside temperatures and high solar-produced temperatures will further improve their desirability. In general, the solar-assisted heat pump system looks good for areas of the country that have a high heating requirement, such as the Northeast and Great Lakes regions.

ABSORPTION COOLING

Solar-assisted air conditioning can be accomplished using absorption refrigeration machines. Perhaps you may recall the refrigerators that operated from a gas flame. These were made by the Servel Company, which later became the Arkansas-Louisiana Gas Company called *Arkla*. Arkla-Servel manufactures a residential size gas-fired air conditioner that has been converted to use solar heat, instead of gas, to drive the unit. This is called an *absorption* machine, and this particular model uses lithium bromide to absorb the refrigerant vapor, changing it to liquid.

Changing refrigerant from vapor to liquid and vapor again is the basic cycle that causes cooling. Conventional air conditioners or refrigerators accomplish this using a mechanical compressor rather than an absorptive chemical.

The important thing to remember is that the solar-heated water from storage replaces natural gas as a heat supply to the unit, and much higher water temperatures are required to operate the air-conditioning unit efficiently.

Although various ranges are quoted, Arkla's literature recommends a hot-water inlet temperature of 210°F for the three-ton (36,000 Btu/h) residential model. This unit will operate with water temperatures of 180°F, but with vastly reduced performance. These units are expensive (approximately $3000 for the Arkla model 501-WF), and the requirement for a water temperature of 210°F places much higher demands on the solar collectors. While the performance of heat-actuated air conditioners improves with increased water temperatures, the performance of the solar collector declines. Only the most efficient flat plate collectors, using dual glazing and selective surfaces, are suitable for this application.

Advanced collectors of the *evacuated* and *focusing* types offer improved performance, but they are also expensive. If you live in an area where the demand for cooling exceeds that for heating, advanced collectors should prove to be more economical, even with a higher initial cost. There are times when the solar-heated water in the storage tank is below the minimum temperature necessary to operate the absorption air conditioner. When this occurs, an internal heater must be used to boost the water temperature as required. Figure 4-6 provides a schematic representation of the components.

Unless you are the type of person who must be the "first on the block" to have solar air conditioning, it would be my recommendation to wait. New, more efficient, and less expensive concepts are being developed every day, both privately and through government-funded research.

One promising concept is the Rankine solar cooling system. Solar-heated water in the 200°F range is used to vaporize a refrigerant, such as Freon. That, in turn, drives a turbine to operate the compressor in the heat pump. With this device you can cool the home with electricity on a hot, *overcast* day. On a hot, *sunny* day, or where 200°F water is available from the storage tank, solar power replaces the vast majority of electricity needed.

Although these units may not be commercially available for a few years to come, they offer the promise of smaller size and much lower cost than the absorption machines. Based on

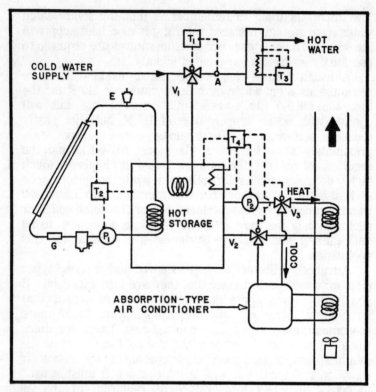

Fig. 4-6. Solar room heating plus hot water and absorption air conditioning.

today's costs and technology, the purchase of a heat-actuated or solar-assisted air conditioner would be difficult to justify on fuel savings alone, and a long payback period should be expected. Most applications you hear about will be for commercial buildings rather than residential buildings.

LOAD PROFILE

In selecting any system combination, full consideration must be given to the specific energy requirements of your home and the climatic conditions in your area. It is helpful to plot a profile of monthly degree days for your specific area, using Table 1-7. A *degree day* is the difference between the average daily temperature and 65°F.

Figure 4-7 is such a plot for Pittsburgh, Pennsylvania. You can see that heating is required nine months out of the year.

The solid-line curve is plotted using the 30-year data collected by the U.S. Weather Bureau and tabulated in Table 1-7. The broken-line curve represents the amount of natural gas used for space heating by the example home of Chapter 1 during 1974.

Although there were some seasonal variations during 1974, such as a mild February and December, there is a good correlation with the historical data. I have not plotted hot water requirements, because they are a relatively small portion of the total and are constant throughout the year. The important point here is to install only what you need to do the job most economically.

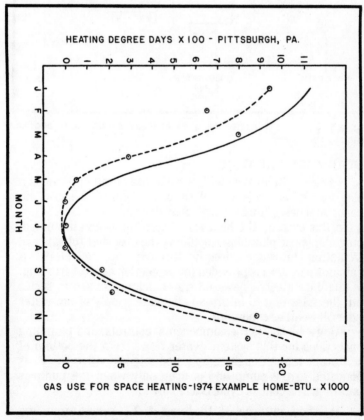

Fig. 4-7. Monthly profile of anticipated and actual heating loads for a Pittsburgh, Pennsylvania residence.

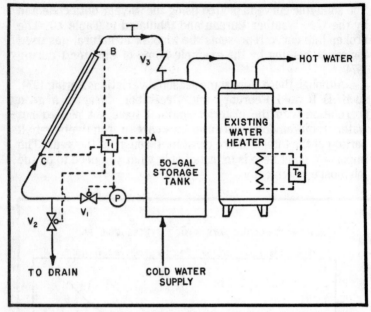

Fig. 4-8. Solar water heater using an auxiliary storage tank and an automatic drain control.

SOLAR WATER HEATER

If you live in an area with a moderate climate, perhaps a solar water heater is your best buy. Figure 4-8 shows an economical design that is worth considering.

In this system, the heat exchanger has been eliminated, using all-copper plumbing (including the absorber tubes), and circulating tapwater directly through the collectors. A drain-down system is provided for protection against freezing. An auxiliary electric-powered water heater is used in series with the solar unit to insure an adequate supply of hot water under all weather conditions.

Figure 4-8 shows the components, controls, and plumbing connections for this system. Water flows from the bottom of the storage tank through pump P and solenoid valve V_1. V_1 is connected to the pump and is open only when the pump is operating. The control cycle is as follows:

1) When differential thermostat T_1 senses that the temperature at point B is 20° higher than that at point A, pump P is turned on, and solar collection begins.

2) When the collectors boost the storage temperature at point A to 140°F, the pump is turned off.

3) With the pump stopped and solenoid valve V_1 closed, if the sensor at point C measures a temperature below 38°F, solenoid valve V_2 is opened, draining the water from the collector loop.

4) If the solar-heated water flowing into the existing water heater is unable to maintain a tank temperature of 140°F, thermostat T_2 activates the electric resistance coil in the unit, boosting the temperature.

V_3 is a check valve to prevent reverse flow; V_4 is an air relief valve, allowing air back into the line to improve draining during the freeze-prevention operation (3).

This system arrangement provides good efficiency; the separate storage tank allows hot water to be collected independent of its use. When the weather is too poor to provide 140°F water, the unit serves as a preheater for the backup or conventional water heater. If you live in an area that has a moderate climate, I recommend this system with single glazing on the collector.

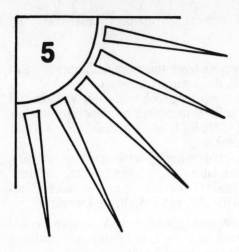

What Size System?

By using the procedure described in Chapter 1, the annual space heating load for a specific house was calculated and found to be 95,220,000 Btu. During the heating season, which is generally defined as October through April, the house used 90,873,000 Btu. This figure, then converted into a heating bill and multiplied by the solar factor for a specific geographic region, provided a guideline for further considering the use of solar energy, which I call the *suitability index*.

Assuming that you have decided to go ahead, more accurate calculations for sizing the system should be made. These will be an approximation, at best, and are not intended to make you a solar "designer" or engineer. But they should provide you with enough knowledge to evaluate claims made by the solar energy firms from which you may be considering making your purchase.

CALCULATION OF COLLECTOR AREA

There are four factors that must be known before an approximation of the collector area can be made. These are:

(1) Btu needed to heat the house.
(2) Amount of solar energy available.
(3) Operating efficiency of the collector.
(4) Percentage of the heating load that solar energy must provide.

How Many Btu Are Needed?

The Btu needed to heat the house can be determined by analyzing the fuel bills as explained in Chapter 1. For a calculation of both collector and storage areas, data for the month of January should be used, for this is typically the most severe month of the heating season.

One word of caution is necessary, however. You should be sure that the particular month used for measurement was not a "freak." You want a typical January, not one representing unusually mild or severe conditions. Ask your local weather station to provide the heating degree days recorded in January for the year your data was taken, then refer to Table 1-7 for the historical reading. If they are close, no adjustment is necessary. But if these readings vary by more than 10%, I suggest that you correct your January fuel use accordingly. For example, if your data for January, 1975, and the weather bureau's degree day reading for that year was 18% below the typical one in Table 1-7, multiply the Btu you calculated by 1.18 (representing an increase of 18%).

In Chapter 1, *heating degree days* were defined as the number of degrees the daily average temperature is below 65°F. A day with an average temperature of 50°F has 15 heating degree days (65 − 50 = 15), while one with an average temperature of 65°F or higher has none. This statistic is also useful for comparing the seasonal fuel requirements in different locations. For example, it would require roughly four and a half times as much fuel to heat a building in Chicago, Illinois as for the same building if it were located in New Orleans, Louisiana.

Available Solar Energy

Once you know how many Btu are needed to heat your specific house, the next step is to calculate the amount of solar energy available. Start with the *mean daily solar radiation* value for your city for the month of January, shown in Table 1-4. This will be in a unit called the langley. All calculations are generally made in Btu, so the langley value must be multiplied by 3.69 (there are 3.69 Btu contained in each langley). This product then provides the average usable solar radiation, both direct and diffuse, falling on a horizontal surface each day, for a specific month and location.

As the arc of the sun is not directly overhead, except at the equator, the solar collectors should be inclined to permit more

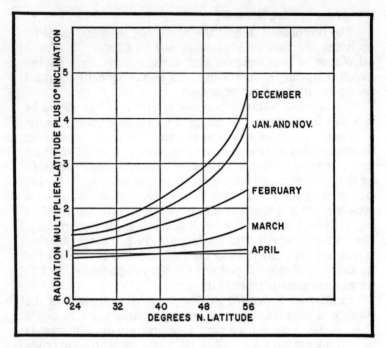

Fig. 5-1. Relative radiation falling on south-facing collectors inclined at latitude plus 10°.

efficient collection. (Although there is not complete agreement as to whether the optimum angle of inclination for the heating season is latitude plus 15° or latitude plus 10°, I have chosen 10° for this text.) To correct radiation data for collectors inclined at latitude plus 10°, the radiation falling on a horizontal surface previously calculated should be multiplied by the radiation multiplier indicated in Fig. 5-1.

For example, if your home is 40° north latitude for the month of January, a collector inclined at 50° (latitude plus 10°) would see twice as much solar radiation as one mounted horizontally or flat. (The radiation multiplier in this case is 2).

The chart in Fig. 5-1 was constructed from tabular data contained in the 1974 ASHRAE Handbook and Product Directory, Applications Volume. This data has been included in Table 5-1, with the permission of ASHRAE. You may wish to refer to it to calculate the effect of collector angles other than 10°, or for applications utilizing combined solar cooling and heating.

Table 5-1. Total Solar Irradiation for a Given Angle

DATE	DEGREES LATITUDE (L)	TILT ANGLE OF SURFACE					
		Horiz. (0°)	L − 10°	L	L + 10°	L + 20°	Vert. (90°)
Jan. 21	24	1622	1984	2174	2300	2360	1766
	32	1288	1839	2008	2118	2166	1779
	40	948	1660	1810	1906	1944	1726
	48	596	1360	1478	1550	1578	1478
	56	282	934	1010	1058	1074	1044
	64	45	268	290	302	306	304
Feb. 21	24	1998	2276	2396	2446	2424	1476
	32	1724	2188	2300	2345	2322	1644
	40	1414	2060	2162	2202	2176	1730
	48	1080	1880	1972	2024	1978	1720
	56	740	1640	1716	1792	1716	1598
	64	400	1230	1286	1302	1282	1252
March 21	24	2270	2428	2456	2412	2298	1022
	32	2084	2378	2403	2358	2246	1276
	40	1852	2308	2330	2284	2174	1484
	48	1578	2208	2228	2182	2074	1632
	56	1268	2066	2084	2040	1938	1700
	64	932	1856	1870	1830	1736	1656
April 21	24	2454	2458	2374	2228	2016	488
	32	2390	2444	2356	2206	1994	764
	40	2274	2412	2320	2168	1956	1022
	48	2106	2358	2266	2114	1902	1262
	56	1892	2282	2186	2038	1830	1450
	64	1644	2776	2082	1936	1736	1594
May 21	24	2556	2447	2286	2072	1800	246
	32	2582	2454	2284	2064	1788	469
	40	2552	2442	2264	2040	1760	724
	48	2482	2418	2234	2010	1728	982
	56	2374	2374	2188	1962	1682	1218
	64	2236	2312	2124	1898	1624	1436
June 21	24	2574	2422	2230	1992	1700	204
	32	2634	2436	2234	1990	1690	370
	40	2648	2434	2224	1974	1670	610
	48	2626	2420	2204	1950	1644	874
	56	2562	2388	2166	1910	1606	1120
	64	2488	2342	2118	1862	1558	1356
July 21	24	2526	2412	2250	2036	1766	246
	32	2558	2442	2250	2030	1754	458
	40	2534	2409	2230	2006	1728	702
	48	2474	2386	2200	1974	1694	956
	56	2372	2342	2152	1926	1646	1186
	64	2248	2280	2090	1864	1588	1400
Aug. 21	24	2408	2402	2316	2168	1958	470
	32	2352	2388	2296	2144	1934	736
	40	2244	2354	2258	2104	1894	978
	48	2086	2300	2200	2046	1836	1208
	56	1883	2218	2118	1966	1760	1392
	64	1646	2108	1008	1860	1662	1522
Sept. 21	24	2194	2432	2366	2322	2212	992
	32	2014	2288	2308	2264	2154	1226
	40	1788	2210	2228	2182	2074	1416
	38	1522	2102	2118	2070	1966	1546
	56	1220	1950	1962	1918	1820	1594
	64	892	1726	1736	1696	1608	1532

Table 5-1. (Continued)

DATE	DEGREES LATITUDE (L)	TILT ANGLE OF SURFACE					
		Horiz (0°)	L − 10°	L	L + 10°	L + 20°	Vert. (90°)
Oct. 21	24	1928	2198	2314	2364	2346	1442
	32	1654	2100	2208	2252	2232	1588
	40	1348	1962	2060	2098	2074	1654
	48	1022	1774	1860	1890	1866	1626
	56	688	1516	1586	1612	1588	1480
	64	358	1088	1136	1152	1134	1106
Nov. 21	24	1610	1962	2146	2268	2324	1730
	32	1280	1816	1980	2084	2130	1742
	40	942	1636	1778	1870	1908	1686
	48	596	1336	1448	1518	1544	1442
	56	284	914	986	1032	1046	1016
	64	46	266	286	298	302	300
Dec. 21	24	1474	1852	2058	2204	2286	1808
	32	1136	1704	1888	2016	2086	1794
	40	782	1480	1634	1740	1796	1646
	48	446	1136	1250	1326	1364	1304
	56	157	620	678	716	734	722
	64	2	20	22	24	24	24

Table 5-1 supplies the day-long direct solar irradiation, in Btu/ft^2, for the twenty-first day of each month, at latitudes from 24° to 64° north, on surfaces normal to the rays of the sun. The total irradiation on horizontal surfaces and south-facing surfaces are given for the following angles, tilted above the horizontal: L − 10°; degrees of latitude (L); L + 10°; L + 20°; and 90° (vertical).

The *radiation multiplier* is calculated by dividing the total solar irradiation for the inclination chosen by that shown in the *horizontal* column. For example, for 40° latitude during June, and with the collector inclined at 50° (L + 10°), the multiplier equals 1974 divided by 2648, or 0.75.

Notice that the collector angle becomes more important as latitude increases. Also, December is the most critical month. Seventy-five percent of the existing houses in the United States are facing the wrong way for optimum solar collection, so chances are you will not have a roof surface facing due south on which collectors can be mounted. If not, you will need to know what effect a change in orientation will have on collection capability. You can deviate up to 45° either east or west of south before a dramatic loss of performance is predicted. If you live in an area having typically overcast mornings, an orientation biased 10° to 15° to the west of south is preferable. Conversely, if cloudy afternoons are typical and you have a choice, face the collectors 10° to 15° east of south for best results. While Table 5-1 gives the theoretical solar irradiation, it does not include the effects of cloud cover. The values given in Table 5-2 provide the percentage of possible sunshine that would actually reach the solar collectors. To estimate the mean daily solar radiation, multiply the total solar irradiation, calculated from Table 5-1, by the factor for your city, provided in Table 5-2.

The effect of cloud cover on the total amount of solar radiation reaching your area is graphically illustrated in Fig. 5-2, which shows the mean percentage of possible sunshine, and Fig. 5-3, which shows the mean total hours of sunshine.

By correlating between Tables 5-1 and 5-2 and Figs. 5-2 and 5-3, you should be able to determine the actual amount of solar radiation for your area, and thereby design your system accordingly.

The next consideration, *collector efficiency*, is the one most likely to be overstated by system salesmen. The federal government recognizes this and is making a strong effort to come up with a national performance standard and rating procedure. Unfortunately, this is at least a couple of years away, in my opinion. In the meantime, the rule is *let the buyer beware*.

It is important to have the best guide possible against which such claims may be measured. In Chapter 3, the effects of selective absorber coatings and the number of covers were discussed. In Figs. 5-4 and 5-5, these variables are plotted, showing collector efficiency for various combinations as a function of temperature difference. These curves were drawn from data provided by Arthur D. Little, Inc., an international management consulting, research, product development, and engineering organization.

It is important to note that collector efficiency decreases rapidly as the temperature difference (the absorber temperature minus the outside air temperature) increases. The collectors in Fig. 5-5, described as "flat-black, unevacuated," have absorbers coated with flat-black paint, which is nonselective (absorptance and emittance are equal). Also, the inside of the collector is at atmospheric pressure (no vacuum). You can see the advantages of a selective surface

Table 5-2. Mean Percentage of Possible Sunshine for Selected Locations

STATE AND STATION	YEARS	JAN.	FEB.	MER.	APR.	MAY	JUNE	JULY	AUG.	SEPT.	OCT.	NOV.	DEC.	ANNUAL
ALABAMA														
Birmingham	56	43	49	56	63	66	67	62	65	66	67	58	44	59
Montgomery	49	51	53	61	69	73	72	66	69	69	71	64	48	64
ALASKA														
Anchorage	19	39	46	56	58	50	51	45	39	35	32	33	29	45
Fairbanks	20	34	50	61	68	55	53	45	35	31	28	38	29	44
Juneau	14	30	32	39	37	34	35	28	30	25	18	21	18	30
Nome	29	44	46	48	53	51	48	32	26	34	35	36	30	41
ARIZONA														
Phoenix	64	76	79	83	88	93	94	84	84	89	88	84	77	85
Yuma	52	83	87	91	94	97	98	92	91	93	93	90	83	91
ARKANSAS														
Little Rock	66	44	53	57	62	67	72	71	73	71	74	58	47	62
CALIFORNIA														
Eureka	49	40	44	50	53	54	56	51	46	52	48	42	39	49
Fresno	55	46	63	72	83	89	94	97	97	93	87	73	47	78
Los Angeles	63	70	69	70	67	68	69	80	81	80	76	79	72	73
Red Bluff	39	50	60	65	75	79	86	95	94	89	77	64	50	75
Sacramento	48	44	57	67	76	82	90	96	95	92	82	65	44	77
San Diego	68	68	67	68	66	60	60	67	70	70	70	76	71	68
San Francisco	64	53	57	63	69	70	75	68	63	70	70	62	54	66
COLORADO														
Denver	64	67	67	65	63	61	69	68	68	71	71	67	65	67
Grand Junction	57	58	62	64	67	71	79	76	72	77	74	67	58	69
CONNECTICUT														
Hartford	48	46	55	56	54	57	60	62	60	57	55	46	46	56
DISTRICT OF COLUMBIA	66	46	53	56	57	61	64	64	62	62	61	54	47	58
FLORIDA														
Apalachicola	26	59	62	62	71	77	70	64	63	62	74	66	53	65
Jacksonville	60	58	59	66	71	71	63	62	63	58	58	61	53	62
Key West	45	68	75	78	78	76	70	69	71	65	65	69	66	71
Miami Beach	48	66	72	73	73	68	62	65	67	62	62	65	65	67
Tampa	63	63	67	71	74	75	66	61	64	64	67	67	61	68
GEORGIA														
Atlanta	65	48	53	57	65	68	68	63	65	67	67	60	47	60.
HAWAII														
Hilo	9	48	42	41	34	31	41	44	38	42	41	34	36	39
Honolulu	53	62	64	60	62	64	66	67	70	70	68	63	60	65
Lihue	9	48	48	48	46	51	60	58	59	67	58	51	49	54
IDAHO														
Boise	20	40	48	59	67	68	75	89	86	81	66	46	37	66
Pocatello	21	37	47	58	64	66	72	82	81	78	66	48	36	64
ILLINOIS														
Cairo	30	46	53	59	65	71	77	82	79	75	73	56	46	65
Chicago	66	44	49	53	56	63	69	73	70	65	61	47	41	59
Springfield	59	47	51	54	58	64	69	76	72	73	64	53	45	60
INDIANA														
Evansville	48	42	49	55	61	67	73	78	76	73	67	52	42	64
Ft. Wayne	48	38	44	51	55	62	69	74	69	64	58	41	38	57
Indianapolis	63	41	47	49	55	62	68	74	70	68	64	48	39	59
IOWA														
Des Moines	66	56	56	56	59	62	66	75	70	64	64	53	48	62
Dubuque	54	48	52	52	58	60	63	73	67	61	55	44	40	57
Sioux City	52	55	58	58	59	63	67	75	72	67	65	53	50	63
KANSAS														
Concordia	52	60	60	62	63	65	73	79	76	72	70	64	58	67
Dodge City	70	67	66	68	68	68	74	78	76	75	70	67	67	71
Wichita	46	61	63	64	64	66	73	80	77	73	69	67	59	69
KENTUCKY														
Louisville	59	41	47	52	57	64	68	72	69	68	64	51	39	59
LOUISIANA														
New Orleans	69	49	50	57	63	66	64	58	60	64	70	60	46	59
Shreveport	18	48	54	58	60	69	78	79	80	79	77	65	60	69
MAINE														
Eastport	58	45	51	52	52	51	53	55	57	54	50	37	40	50
MASSACHUSETTS														
Boston	67	47	56	57	56	59	62	64	63	61	58	48	48	57
MICHIGAN														
Alpena	45	29	43	52	56	59	64	70	64	52	44	24	22	51
Detroit	69	34	42	48	52	58	65	69	66	61	54	35	29	53
Grand Rapids	56	26	37	48	54	60	66	72	67	58	50	31	22	49
Marquette	55	31	40	47	52	53	56	63	57	47	38	24	24	47
S. Ste. Marie	60	28	44	50	54	54	59	63	58	45	36	21	22	47
MINNESOTA														
Duluth	49	47	55	60	58	58	60	68	63	53	47	36	40	55
Minneapolis	45	49	54	55	57	60	64	72	69	60	54	40	40	56
MISSISSIPPI														
Vicksburg	66	46	50	57	64	69	73	69	72	74	71	60	45	64
MISSOURI														
Kansas City	69	55	57	59	60	64	70	76	73	70	67	59	52	65
St. Louis	68	48	49	56	59	64	68	72	68	67	65	54	44	61
Springfield	45	48	54	57	60	63	69	77	72	71	65	58	48	63
MONTANA														
Havre	55	49	58	61	63	63	65	78	75	64	57	48	46	62
Helena	65	46	55	58	60	59	63	77	74	63	57	48	43	60
Kalispell	50	28	40	49	57	58	60	77	73	61	50	28	20	53
NEBRASKA														
Lincoln	55	57	59	60	60	63	69	76	71	67	66	59	55	64
North Platte	53	63	63	64	62	64	72	78	74	72	70	62	58	68
NEVADA														
Ely	21	61	64	68	65	67	79	79	81	81	73	67	62	72
Las Vegas	19	74	77	78	81	85	91	84	86	92	84	83	75	82

Table 5-2. (Continued)

STATE AND STATION	YEARS	JAN.	FEB.	MER.	APR.	MAY	JUNE	JULY	AUG.	SEPT.	OCT.	NOV.	DEC.	ANNUAL
Reno	51	59	64	69	75	77	82	90	89	86	76	68	56	76
Winnemucca	53	52	60	64	70	76	83	90	90	86	75	62	53	74
NEW HAMPSHIRE														
Concord	44	48	53	55	53	51	56	57	58	55	50	43	43	52
NEW JERSEY														
Atlantic City	62	51	57	58	59	62	65	67	66	65	54	58	52	60
NEW MEXICO														
Albuquerque	28	70	72	72	76	79	84	76	75	81	80	79	70	76
Roswell	47	69	72	75	77	76	80	76	75	74	74	74	69	74
NEW YORK														
Albany	63	43	51	53	53	57	62	63	61	58	54	39	38	53
Binghamton	63	31	39	41	44	50	56	54	51	47	43	29	26	44
Buffalo	49	32	41	49	51	59	67	70	67	60	51	31	28	53
Canton	43	37	47	50	48	54	61	63	61	54	45	30	31	49
New York	83	49	56	57	59	62	65	66	64	61	54	53	50	59
Syracuse	49	31	38	45	50	58	64	67	63	56	47	29	26	50
NORTH CAROLINA														
Asheville	57	48	53	56	61	64	63	59	59	62	64	59	48	58
Raleigh	61	50	56	59	64	67	65	62	62	63	64	62	52	61
NORTH DAKOTA														
Bismarck	65	52	58	56	57	58	61	73	69	62	59	49	48	59
Devils Lake	55	53	60	59	60	59	62	71	67	59	56	44	45	58
Fargo	39	47	55	56	58	62	63	73	69	60	57	39	46	59
Williston	43	51	59	60	63	66	66	78	75	65	60	48	48	63
OHIO														
Cincinnati	44	41	46	52	56	62	69	72	68	68	60	46	39	57
Cleveland	65	29	36	45	52	61	67	71	68	62	54	32	25	50
Columbus	65	36	44	49	54	63	68	71	68	66	60	44	35	55
OKLAHOMA														
Okla. City	62	57	60	63	64	65	74	78	78	74	68	64	57	68
OREGON														
Baker	46	41	49	56	61	63	67	83	81	74	62	46	37	60
Portland	69	27	34	41	49	52	55	70	65	55	42	28	23	48
Roseburg	29	24	32	40	51	57	59	79	77	68	42	28	18	51
PENNSYLVANIA														
Harrisburg	60	43	52	55	57	61	65	68	63	62	58	47	43	57
Philadelphia	66	45	56	57	58	61	62	64	61	62	61	53	49	57
Pittsburgh	63	32	39	45	50	57	62	64	61	62	54	39	30	51
RHODE ISLAND														
Block Island	48	45	54	47	56	58	60	62	62	60	59	50	44	56
SOUTH CAROLINA														
Charleston	61	58	60	65	72	73	70	66	66	67	68	68	57	66
Columbia	55	53	57	62	68	69	68	63	65	64	68	64	51	63
SOUTH DAKOTA														
Huron	62	55	62	60	62	65	68	76	72	66	61	52	49	63
Rapid City	53	58	62	63	62	61	66	73	73	69	66	58	54	64
TENNESSEE														
Knoxville	62	42	49	53	59	64	66	64	59	64	64	53	41	57
Memphis	55	44	51	57	64	68	74	73	74	70	69	58	45	64
Nashville	63	42	47	54	60	65	69	69	68	69	65	55	42	59
TEXAS														
Abilene	14	64	68	73	66	73	86	83	85	73	71	72	66	73
Amarillo	54	71	71	75	75	75	82	81	81	79	76	76	70	76
Austin	33	46	50	57	60	62	72	76	79	70	70	57	49	63
Brownsville	37	44	49	51	57	65	73	78	78	67	70	54	44	61
Del Rio	36	53	55	61	63	60	66	75	80	69	66	58	52	63
El Paso	53	74	77	81	85	87	87	78	78	80	82	80	73	80
Ft. Worth	33	56	57	65	66	67	75	78	78	74	70	63	58	68
Galveston	66	50	50	55	61	69	76	72	71	70	74	62	49	63
San Antonio	57	48	51	56	58	60	69	74	75	69	67	55	49	62
UTAH														
Salt Lake City	22	48	53	61	68	73	78	82	82	84	73	56	49	69
VERMONT														
Burlington	54	34	43	48	47	53	59	62	59	51	43	25	24	46
VIRGINIA														
Norfolk	60	50	57	60	63	67	66	66	66	63	64	60	51	62
Richmond	56	49	55	59	63	67	66	65	62	63	64	58	50	61
WASHINGTON														
North Head	44	28	37	42	48	48	48	50	46	48	41	31	27	41
Seattle	26	27	34	42	48	53	48	62	56	53	36	28	24	45
Spokane	62	26	41	53	63	64	68	82	79	68	53	28	22	58
Tatoosh Island	49	26	36	39	45	47	46	48	44	47	38	26	23	40
Walla Walla	44	24	35	51	63	67	72	86	84	72	59	33	20	60
Yakima	18	34	49	62	70	72	74	86	86	74	61	38	29	65
WEST VIRGINIA														
Elkins	55	33	37	42	47	55	55	56	53	55	51	41	33	48
Parkersburg	62	30	36	42	49	56	60	63	60	60	53	37	29	48
WISCONSIN														
Green Bay	57	44	51	55	56	58	64	70	65	58	52	40	40	55
Madison	59	44	49	52	53	58	64	70	66	60	56	41	38	56
Milwaukee	59	44	48	53	56	60	65	73	67	62	56	44	39	57
WYOMING														
Cheyenne	63	65	66	64	61	59	68	70	68	69	69	65	63	66
Lander	57	66	70	71	66	65	74	76	75	72	67	61	62	69
Sheridan	52	56	61	62	61	61	67	76	74	67	60	53	52	64
Yellowstone Park	35	39	51	55	57	56	63	73	71	65	57	45	38	56
PUERTO RICO														
San Juan	57	64	69	71	66	59	62	65	67	61	63	63	65	65

Climatic Atlas of the United States, U.S. Department of Commerce

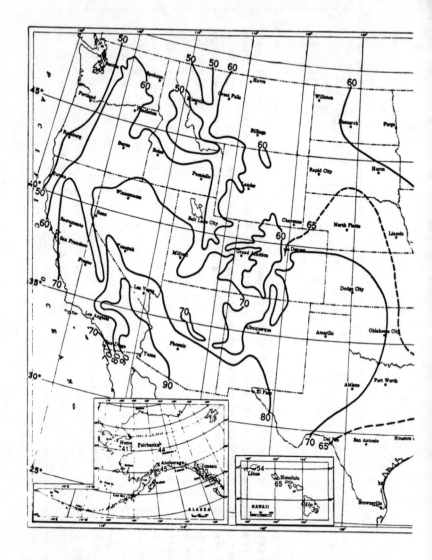

and vacuum as the temperature requirements become greater.

In Chapter 3 it was stated that, in general, effective operating temperatures for working fluids are 140°F for space or room heating, 150°F for domestic hot water, and 220°F for absorption-type air conditioning. The average temperature of the absorber should be approximately 20° higher than these

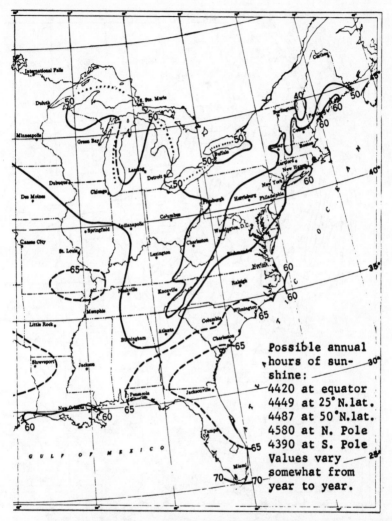

Possible annual
hours of sun-
shine:
4420 at equator
4449 at 25° N. lat.
4487 at 50° N. lat.
4580 at N. Pole
4390 at S. Pole
Values vary
somewhat from
year to year.

Fig. 5-2. Mean percentage of possible sunshine, annual.

values to provide for heat losses, including the effect of the heat exchanger in the collector loop if one is used.

To calculate the temperature difference for a room heating application, use the value for the normal daily average temperature for the month of January for your particular city. (This data for key cities is shown in Table 6-1.) Subtract this value from 140°F (for room heating). Once this temperature

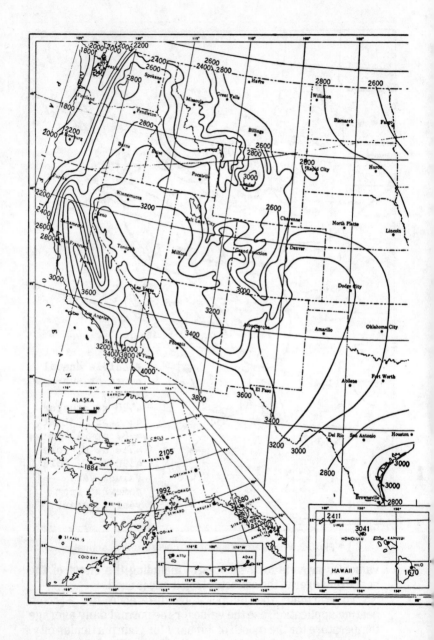

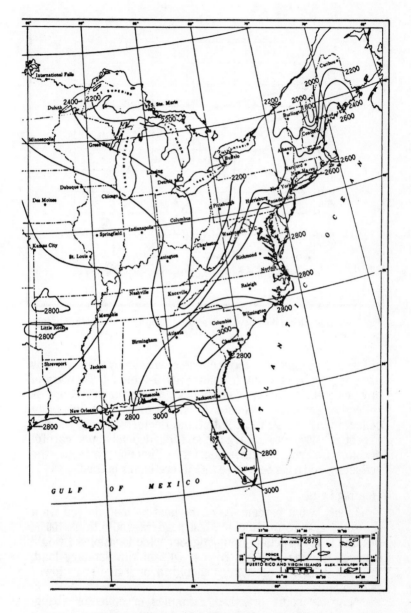

Fig. 5-3. Mean total hours of sunshine, annual.

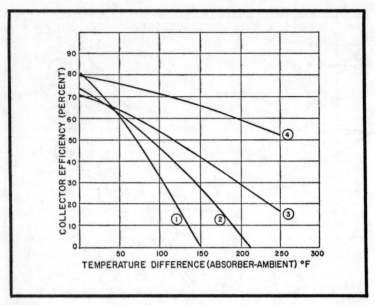

Fig. 5-4. Collector efficiency for various designs and operating temperatures.

difference is known, the collector efficiency for various designs may be calculated, using Figs. 5-4 and 5-5. Be wary of any design that claims an efficiency greater than 60%, unless reflective surfaces are used to supplement the flat plate collector (as in Fig. 3-12). With the reflector, the best you can expect is a 30% insolation gain, and this depends upon careful design. Determine the collector efficiency without the reflector; add a conservative 15% if a reflector is used.

Heating Load

Lastly, what percentage of the heating load do you want the solar system to handle? Most readers would think 100%, but this is not practical in most geographic locations. I would suggest starting with a figure of 50% of the January load, revising it later if economics should favor a higher or lower percentage.

Now for some practical examples of collector sizing. Pursuing the study of the home in Chapter 1, we know it had an energy consumption of 18,837,000 Btu in January. Using this figure, and the data in Tables 5-3 and 5-4, a calculation of

```
┌─────────────────────────────────────────────────────────────┐
│  CONDITIONS AND CHARACTERISTICS OF COLLECTORS TESTED          │
│                                                               │
│      NORMAL INCIDENT RADIATION = 250 BTU/HR-FT²               │
│      AMBIENT AIR TEMPERATURE = 50°F                           │
│      SPACING OF COVER PANES = 0.5 INCH                        │
│                                                               │
│  CURVE    COLLECTOR      NUMBER      ABSORBER PROPERTIES       │
│  (Fig.5-2) DESCRIPTION   OF PANES    ABSORPTANCE  EMITTANCE    │
│                                                               │
│   ①      FLAT-BLACK,       1          0.93        0.93        │
│          UNEVACUATED                                          │
│                                                               │
│   ②      FLAT-BLACK,       2          0.93        0.93        │
│          UNEVACUATED                                          │
│                                                               │
│   ③      SELECTIVE,        2          0.90        0.10        │
│          UNEVACUATED                                          │
│                                                               │
│   ④      SELECTIVE,        1          0.90        0.10        │
│          HIGH VACUUM                                          │
└─────────────────────────────────────────────────────────────┘
```

Fig. 5-5. Description and operating conditions of collectors tested. (Courtesy Arthur D. Little, Inc.)

collector size will be made for both Grand Junction, Colorado and Boston, Massachusetts. For collector efficiency, assume that a double-pane flat plate collector with a selective surface has been chosen, and that the primary function of the system will be for room heating, requiring an average absorber operating temperature of 140°F.

The collector area (A) required for 100% solar dependency can be found by multiplying the monthly collectable energy (in

Table 5-3. Solar Energy Available in January

	Grand Junction	Boston
Langley/day-ft²	227	129
Btu/day-ft²	837	476
Latitude	39°	42°
Collector angle	49°	32°
Radiation multiplier	2.0	2.2
Collectable energy Btu/day-ft²	1674	1047
Collectable energy Btu/month-ft²	51,894	32,457

Table 5-4. Calculation of Collector Efficiency

	Grand Junction	Boston
Average Absorber Temperature	140°F	140°F
Daily Average Outdoor Tempurature (Jan.)	26°F	30°F
Temperature Difference (ΔT)	114°F	110°F
Collector Efficiency	50%	52%

Btu) by the collector efficiency; then, divide this figure into the monthly energy used (in Btu).

For Grand Junction

$$A = \frac{18,837,000}{51,894 \times 0.5} = 726 \text{ sq ft}$$

For Boston

$$A = \frac{18,837,000}{32,457 \times 0.52} = 1116 \text{ sq ft}$$

These figures are for 100% solar dependency, which is not practical, as you will discover in our next analysis on sizing the storage tank.

SIZING THE STORAGE TANK

Again from our example home, the energy required for heating during the month of January is 18,837,000 Btu, or 607,645 Btu daily. If the solar system were required to supply 100% of this energy, and water was used as a storage medium, you would need a storage tank capacity of 973 gallons for each consecutive sunless day. If you experienced a week without sunshine, the storage tank would require a capacity of 6811 gallons—and be 20 ft in diameter and 22 long!

This should demonstrate that it is not practical to store energy for an extended period of time. In addition, the calculation just made makes no provision for heat lost from the storage tank due to incomplete insulation. Even with a well-insulated tank, either buried in the ground or installed in the basement, you should assume that 10% of the storage temperature will be lost each day due to convection, conduction, and radiation.

The best way to attack the problem of storage size is to start with a tank that will supply 50% of the average January heat load over two sunless days. For the example home, the energy required in January is 607,645 Btu per day; 50% of this is 303,823 Btu and, adding 10% for heat losses, the storage capacity must be 334,205 Btu per day. For two sunless days, 668,410 Btu must be provided. The following formula is used to make the calculation on the tank volume:

$$E_s = V \times C_w \times \Delta T$$
where
E_s = energy stored in Btu
V = tank volume in cubic feet
C_w = heat capacity of water in Btu/ft^3-°F
ΔT = difference between the maximum storage temperature and the temperature downpoint

You may recall in Chapter 3, under the section on *Heat Storage Materials*, I defined what is meant by specific heat. The heat capacity of water (C_w) is the specific heat multiplied by density, or 62.4 Btu/ft^3-°F. If you have crushed rock as a storage material, just call its heat capacity C_R and use 21 Btu/ft^3-°F in the formula.

I also want to discuss what is meant by delta T or ΔT. In most systems, the storage tank temperature remains below the collector temperature while fluid is circulating (see Fig. 3-15). In addition, if you use a heat exchanger some heat is lost in the transfer, as the efficiency of exchangers is not 100%. Assume that a maximum storage tank temperature of 160°F is desired. If you use this heated water for room heating, the minimum usable storage temperature is approximately 85°F. This is also called the *downpoint* temperature, or the point at which it is more economical to use the auxiliary heating system rather than pump the solar-heated water through the heat exchanger located above the blower fan. I described this as a typical heating system in Chapter 4. In this case

Maximum storage temperature = 160°F
Downpoint temperature = 85°F
Difference of ΔT = 75°F

Putting this data into the tank volume formula

$$E_s = V \times C_w \times \Delta T$$
$$V = E_s/(C_w \times \Delta T)$$

then, inserting values

$$V = 668,410/(62.4 \times 75)$$
$$= 143 \text{ cu ft}$$

Table 5-5. Conversion Factors

CONVERSION	MULTIPLIER
Btu to kWh	0.00029
Btu/dq ft to langleys (cal/cm^2)	0.271
Btu to calories	252
Btu to therms	0.00001
Calories to Btu	0.00397
Cubic feet to gallons (Y.S.)	7.481
Horsepower to kilowatts (kS)	0.745
Horsepower to Btu	2544
Kilowatt-hours (kWh) to Btu	2413
Langleys to Btu/sq ft	3.69
Refrigeration tons to Btu/hr	12,000
Therm to Btu	100,000

As there are 7.481 gallons of water in each cubic foot (from the conversion table in Table 5-5), the storage tank must hold 1070 gallons to supply enough storage capacity for 50% of the average January heating load for two sunless days.

The most economical storage size depends on several variables: climate, amount of sunshine, solar collector costs, storage tank costs, specific fuel rates for your area, and others. Several researchers have run computer programs on these factors; but most of them are tied to a specific set of conditions, and your home may not fit any of them. The important thing to remember is not to collect and store fluids at a higher tempereture than you *really* need, and don't plan storage for more than a three-day sunless period.

ECONOMIC ANALYSIS

With a knowledge of how to calculate collector and storage areas, the next step is to apply the calculations to your specific case and measure the results. Data should be assembled to plot the Btu per month required to heat your home, and the Btu available per month from the size, type, and orientation of the collector array selected.

Figure 5-6 is such a plot for the example home in Chapter 1 located in Grand Junction, Colorado. The monthly energy required includes the needs of the water heater. A collector area of 423 ft was chosen, representing 50% of the January heating load. The lined area between the curves represents potential fuel savings. You can see that more energy is collected from May through September than required. In some areas, although Grand Junction is not one of them, this could be economically used for solar-assisted air conditioning. The data used in constructing Fig. 5-6 is tabulated in Table 5-6.

If all the energy collected in the lined portion of Fig. 5-6 could be transformed directly into heated air for room heat without losses, the annual fuel bill (in this case, we will assume it is electric) would virtually be eliminated from April through October, and substantially reduced for the balance of the year. Solar systems are not 100% efficient, and you should provide for heat losses from the point of collection to the point of conversion and for the use of the energy.

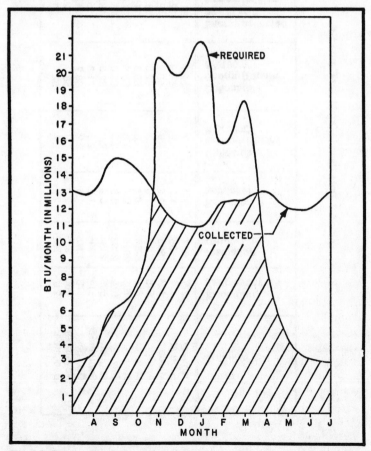

Fig. 5-6. Solar collection and total heating requirements for the example home located in Grand Junction, Colorado.

Table 5-6. Data Used to Construct Figure 5-6

Month	Insolation (langley/day-ft²)	Insolation (Btu/day-ft²)	Radiation Multiplier	Collectable Energy (Btu/day-ft²×1000)	Collectable Energy (Btu/mo. ft²×1000)	Energy collected by 423 sq ft system (million Btu/month)	Energy required (million Btu/month)	Percentage of energy supplied by system
January	227	837	2.0	1.7	52.7	11.1	21.9	50
February	324	1195	1.6	1.9	58.9	12.5	16.0	78
March	434	1600	1.2	1.9	58.9	12.5	18.6	67
April	546	2013	1.0	2.0	62.0	13.1	8.8	100
May	615	2268	0.8	1.8	55.8	11.8	4.1	100
June	708	2610	0.7	1.8	55.8	11.8	3.2	100
July	676	2493	0.8	2.0	62.0	13.1	3.1	100
August	595	2194	0.9	2.0	62.0	13.1	3.2	100
September	514	1895	1.2	2.3	71.3	15.1	6.3	100
October	373	1375	1.6	2.2	68.2	14.4	7.3	100
November	260	959	2.0	1.9	58.9	12.5	20.7	60
December	212	782	2.2	1.7	52.7	11.1	19.9	56

Collector efficiency has already been accounted for, but you should also consider line losses, tank losses, and heat-exchanger inefficiencies. I know of no scientific way to calculate these without examining each individual system for the thickness and quality of insulation used, the storage tank location, and the heat-exchanger performance curves. I will give you a rule of thumb, but keep in mind it is just that. *Assume that a well-designed system using flat plate collectors can deliver 90% of the energy collected in usable form to apply against the load.* There isn't such a thing as a 100% efficient heating system, either solar, electric, gas, or fuel oil. Beware of a salesman who claims he has one!

Pursuing the economics, if you discount the solar energy collected by 10% and calculate the annual saving in Btu and dollars, you can estimate how many years it would take to pay off a given system based on present and future energy costs. Let's complete the example for the Grand Junction, Colorado residence in Table 5-7.

Table 5-7. Annual Totals Used With Figure 5-6

Month	Energy required (million Btumonth)	Ninety percent of energy collected by 423 sq ft system (million Btumonth)	Million Btumonth saved by using solar system	kWh saved by using solar system	Savings based on rate of 3.36¢/kWh
January	21.9	10.0	11.9	3487	$117
February	16.0	11.3	4.7	1377	46
March	18.6	11.3	7.3	2138	72
April	8.8	11.8	8.8	2578	87
May	4.1	10.6	4.1	1201	40
June	3.2	10.6	3.2	937	31
July	3.1	11.8	3.1	908	31
August	3.2	11.8	3.2	937	31
September	6.3	13.6	6.3	1845	62
October	7.3	13.0	7.3	2138	72
November	20.7	11.3	9.4	2753	93
December	19.9	10.0	9.9	2900	97
Annual Total	133.1	137.1	79.2	23,200	$779

Table 5-8. Fuel Cost Increasing at 4% Compounded Annually

Year	Fuel Cost (γkWh)	Yearly Savings ($)	Cumulative Savings ($)
1 (1975)	3.36	779	779
2	3.49	810	1589
3	3.63	842	2431
4	3.78	887	3308
5	3.93	912	4220
6	4.09	949	5169
7	4.25	986	6155
8	4.42	1025	7180
9	4.60	1067	8247
10	4.78	1109	9356
11	4.97	1153	10,509

Suppose you have selected a system that costs $20 per square foot, including installation. In this case, for 423 sq ft the system cost is $8460. At an annual savings of $779, it would take 10.9 years to pay off. This is at the 3.36¢ per kWh rate. If you assume the cost of electricity will continue to escalate (as most people assume), you should refigure this payback period based upon a compound annual percentage of fuel increase.

Tables 5-8 and 5-9 show the differences in cost when fuel prices rise at a rate of 4% annually (Table 5-8) as compared to when they rise at a rate of 8% annually (Table 5-9).

Considering fuel-cost escalations, the system would be paid off in just over 8 years at 4%, and just over 9 years at 8%. From that point on, the annual savings are yours. But there are

Table 5-9. Fuel Cost Increasing at 8% Compounded Annually

Year	Fuel Cost (γkWh)	Yearly Savings ($)	Cumulative Savings ($)
1 (1975)	3.36	779	779
2	3.63	842	1621
3	3.92	909	2530
4	4.23	981	3511
5	4.57	1060	4571
6	4.94	1153	5724
7	5.33	1237	6961
8	5.76	1336	8297
9	6.22	1443	9740
10	6.72	1559	11,299
11	7.25	1682	12,981

those who would challenge this evaluation as not being complete. For example, you could have your $8460 invested in savings and earning interest, therefore this interest that could have been earned should be deducted from the calculated savings. In addition, the system will require some annual maintenance, and this should also be deducted.

But what about the fact that the system has increased the value of your home? And that a portion of its price can be recaptured upon sale if the system is kept in good working order? Also, there may be federal, state, and county tax advantages to owning and operating a solar heater.

I believe this may be the case, and these factors should balance out. You can be confused by all these unknowns, and I recommend that, if you like the annual fuel savings predicted, you should make the investment. But be sure the system will perform as warranted and outlast its mortgage.

6

Solar Water Heaters

If you discuss the principle of solar water heating with long-time residents of Florida, they will be quick to tell you that the concept is not new. In fact, this Florida industry grew at an exceptional pace between 1936 and 1941. During the war, sales tapered off due to material shortages; and in 1950, the once flourishing business began its decline. There were sound reasons why this happened, and I thing it is important for you to know them in order to avoid mistakes made in the past.

First, let's note that the economics of operation must exist before a large-scale demand can develop. As natural gas was not available in the Miami area until 1959, homeowners had only two choices for heating water: electricity or solar energy. In 1936, residential electric rates averaged over 5¢ per kWh, but this rate fell to just over 3¢ per kWh in 1950. Concurrently, the cost of manufacturing and installing the solar units doubled, then tripled, with increased labor and material costs.

The solar energy business was basically confined to small shops, having little opportunity to reduce costs through large volume, and more labor was required to install the type of units being sold. It should be apparent then, from our analysis in Chapter 5, that the payback period, or the time it would take a homeowner to recapture his initial investment, extended beyond the number of years he was willing to wait.

A second problem the industry faced was that many firms selling these solar units gave little thought to engineering them. Many homeowners complained that a sufficient amount of hot water was not available from the solar units. An even greater credibility problem occurred as storage tanks developed leaks and needed replacement. Many of these tanks were roof mounted units disguised to look like chimneys. They were built into the attic structure; when leaks occurred, the water ran into the house. Replacement costs wiped out fuel savings, and some marginal operators could not be located to even discuss the problem. It didn't take long for news like this to travel and discourage new sales.

I'm sure, at this point, you have developed some serious concerns about the advantages of owning a solar water heater—and that's good! As long as you're concerned enough to investigate and question the purchase, you will make the sales job difficult for "fast buck" opportunists who are starting to invade the solar energy industry. As the marketing opportunity for solar water heaters is more immediate than for space heating and cooling applications, I would expect to see them enter this field first.

What has changed since the demise of the Florida market? You might say *everything* and *nothing*. There are still firms that don't do their engineering homework, ignoring the effects of dissimilar metals and the resulting corrosion that caused many of those tank failures in Florida (see Chapter 3 under *Storage Tanks* for precautions). And there are salesmen who overstate the capabilities of their systems in order to sell their units. The major difference is that the potential of solar energy, coupled with irritation over rising utility bills, has triggered a national development program, resulting in many solid designs by established firms from which you may choose.

TYPES OF SYSTEMS

Solar water heaters fall into four broad classifications:

- Thermosiphon systems
- Pumped systems.
- Heat exchanged systems
- Preheaters with supplemental storage

There can be combinations of these four classes, but let's start by describing the operating principles of each system individually.

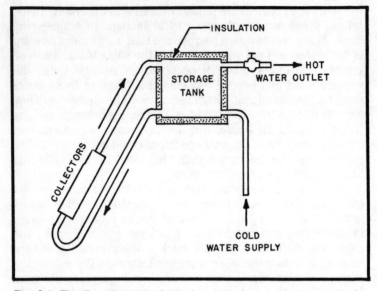

Fig. 6-1. The flow diagram of a solar water heater, operating on the thermosiphon principle.

Thermosiphon Systems

In a *thermosiphon* system, the storage tank is located above the solar collectors. If the top of the collector is one to two feet below the bottom of the storage tank, and the connecting lines are well insulated, heated water should flow upward into the storage tank and be replaced by colder water with increased density. With the proper system design, this flow occurs without the aid of a pump, and it will not reverse at night when the collectors cool off.

Figure 6-1 describes the flow path. This is the type of system used in most early Florida installations and presently quite popular in Australia. As you can see from the figure, cold water is supplied at city main pressure, which can be up to 100 lb/sq in. All connections and components must be capable of withstanding at least this much pressure.

In this most basic system, tapwater is circulated through the collector. Impurities in the water may be deposited inside the absorber tubes over the years, causing less heat transfer and reduced performance. The rate at which deposits form is a function of your local water conditions; it may not happen at all, but you should at least be alert to the possibility.

The collectors and storage tank should be in close proximity, and be either ground mounted, as in Fig. 6-2, or roof mounted, as in Fig. 6-3. Each location has advantages and disadvantages that must be considered. On the ground, collectors are subject to more shading from such things as shrubs and trees, and possible damage by vandalism. Roof mounted units cause major problems if they leak (as many did in early Florida installations), and you must compensate for increased structural loads on the roof and roof trusses.

Pumped Systems

Adding a pump to the collector loop, which I will call a *pumped system*, increases both initial costs and operating costs, but provides more flexibility. In the basic plumbing shown in Fig. 6-4, it is not necessary to mount the storage tank higher than the collector, and the rate of flow of water through the collectors (and thus their efficiency) can be varied by pump selection and speed control.

Heat Exchanged Systems

The principles of a *heat exchanged* system have been described throughout this book, so I will not repeat them here.

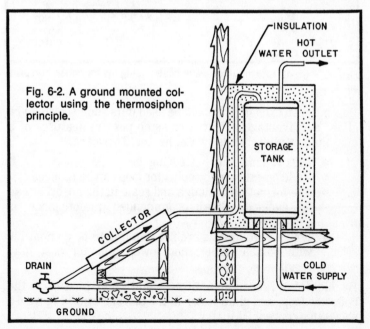

Fig. 6-2. A ground mounted collector using the thermosiphon principle.

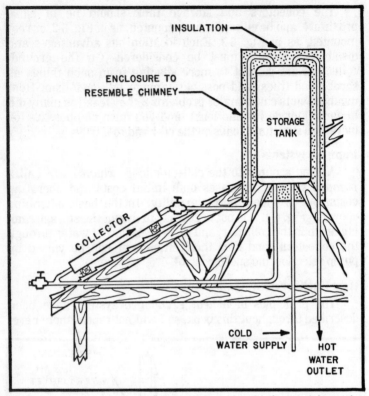

Fig. 6-3. A typical roof mounted water heater using the thermosiphon principle.

Basically, an exchanger should be used if its added cost can be offset by advantages. There are some positive features of a dual-fluid, heat-exchanged water heater. These are:

- Less vulnerability to freezing.
- Fluid pressure in the collector loop can be reduced.
- The formation of sludge and scale in the absorber can be avoided when recommended maintenance is performed.
- Collector materials are not required to be compatible with potable water, and lower collector cost may result.

By dual fluid, I mean an antifreeze and water mixture in the collector loop, and plain water in the storage tank. Figure 6-5 shows this concept.

Preheater Systems

Using solar energy to *preheat* water in a supplemental storage tank is a most popular option. Figure 6-6 depicts an arrangement that provides good efficiency, as the separate storage tank allows hot water to be collected independent of its use. Hooked in series with your existing water heater, an adequate supply of hot water is assured under all climatic conditions. The operation of this unit was described in detail in Chapter 4.

Other Systems

Other concepts are available in solar water heaters. In Japan, the Hitachi Company has sold over 200,000 units that

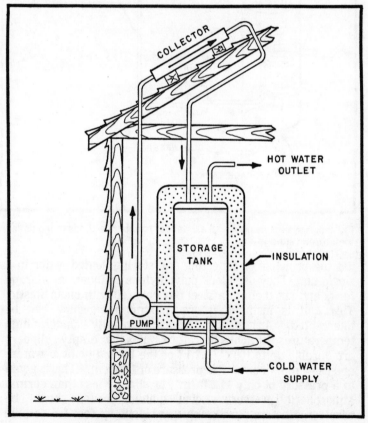

Fig. 6-4. A solar water heater using a circulation pump.

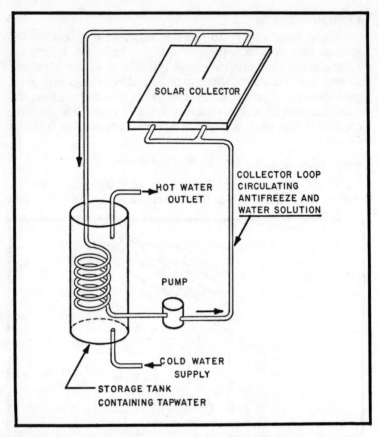

Fig. 6-5. A system using a heat exchanger to separate fluids in the collector loop and storage tank.

use the principle of collecting and storing heated water in a single unit. They use black polyethylene cylinders as *storage tanks* and put them in a steel box covered with clear plastic. This *unit* is installed where maximum sunshine can be intercepted. As plastic deforms readily under high temperatures, Hitachi's literature states that empty cylinders are durable up to 100°C (212°F, or the boiling point of water) and use a maximum water pressure of 1 kg/cm^2. This is equal to a pressure of only 14.2 lb/in^2, or slightly less than normal atmospheric pressure. Local building codes should be considered before purchasing any plastic system for potable water service.

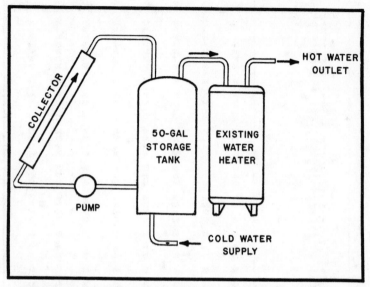

Fig. 6-6. Using solar energy to preheat water. This system provides supplemental storage and automatic drain control for freezing weather conditions. The supplementary solar storage tank is connected in series with a conventional water heater.

LOAD CALCULATIONS

The first design consideration is to determine what the hot-water service load will be. Homeowner preferences for water temperatures vary ranging from 125°F to 180°F. For design purposes throughout this text, it is assumed that 140°F water is required, and that each family member uses 20 gallons per day.

The water heater must raise the water temperature from that of the house supply line to 140°F. It can be assumed that the supply-line temperature is equal to the average daily outdoor temperature (found in Table 6-1), and that the demand for hot water is basically constant throughout the year. As an example, if you have a family of three living in Grand Junction, Colorado, the water heater must deliver 60 gallons per day (20 gallons × 3 family members) and must raise the temperature from the annual average of 52.6°F to 140°F. The energy required in Btu to do this job may be calculated from the following formula:

$$Q = G \times K \times \Delta T$$

Table 6-1. Normal Daily Average Temperature for the Heating Season

CITIES	OCT.	NOV.	DEC.	JAN.	FEB.	MAR.	APR.	AVERAGE (12 MONTHS)
ALASKA								
Anchorage	35	22	14	12	18	23	36	35
Barrow	17	−1	−11	−16	−18	−15	0	10
Cold Bay	40	29	34	28	28	29	33	38
Fairbanks	26	4	−8	−11	−3	9	29	26
Juneau	42	34	28	25	27	30	38	40
Nome	30	17	6	4	6	8	21	26
Shemya	40	36	31	31	31	32	36	38
ALABAMA								
Montgomery	67	54	48	48	50	56	64	65
ARIZONA								
Flagstaff	47	36	30	27	30	36	43	46
Yuma	76	64	57	55	59	66	72	74
ARKANSAS								
Little Rock	63	50	42	41	44	52	62	62
CALIFORNIA								
Eureka	54	51	49	47	48	49	50	52
Fresno	65	54	47	46	51	55	61	63
Los Angeles	65	61	57	54	55	57	59	62
San Francisco	61	55	50	49	51	53	56	57
COLORADO								
Denver	51	38	32	29	32	36	46	50
Grand Junction	55	39	29	26	33	42	52	53
DISTRICT OF COLUMBIA	59	48	38	37	38	45	56	57
FLORIDA								
Jacksonville	71	62	56	56	58	62	69	70
Miami	78	72	68	67	68	71	74	75
Tallahassee	70	57	54	54	56	61	68	68
Tampa	75	67	62	61	63	66	71	72
GEORGIA								
Atlanta	63	51	44	45	47	52	61	62
HAWAII								
Hilo	75	73	72	71	71	71	72	73
Honolulu	78	76	74	73	72	73	74	76
IDAHO								
Boise	52	39	32	29	35	42	50	51
ILLINOIS								
Chicago	55	40	29	26	28	36	49	51
IOWA								
Des Moines	54	37	26	21	24	36	50	50
KANSAS								
Wichita	60	44	36	32	36	45	57	57
LOUISIANA								
New Orleans	70	60	55	55	57	61	68	69
Shreveport	67	55	50	48	50	57	65	66
MAINE								
Caribou	43	30	16	11	13	23	36	39
MASSACHUSETTS								
Boston	55	45	33	30	30	38	48	51
MICHIGAN								
Detroit	54	40	29	27	27	35	48	50
Sault Ste. Marie	46	33	21	16	16	24	38	41
MINNESOTA								
Internat'l Falls	42	24	9	3	7	19	37	36
Minneapolis	48	31	18	12	16	28	45	44
MISSOURI								
St. Louis	59	44	35	32	35	43	55	56
MONTANA								
Glacier Nat'l Park	43	31	26	21	24	31	42	42
Havre	46	30	21	14	16	27	43	42
Miles City	49	33	23	17	20	31	46	46
Missoula	44	31	24	19	25	34	44	43
NEBRASKA								
Lincoln	57	41	30	25	29	38	52	53
North Platte	51	36	27	24	28	35	48	50
NEVADA								
Las Vegas	67	53	45	43	48	55	65	66
Reno	49	38	32	30	36	42	48	49
NEW MEXICO								
Albuquerque	58	44	37	35	40	46	56	57
NEW YORK								
Buffalo	51	39	27	25	24	32	44	47
New York	59	47	36	34	34	41	51	55
NORTH CAROLINA								
Asheville	58	47	40	40	41	46	56	57
Hatteras	65	56	48	47	47	51	59	62
Raleigh	61	50	42	42	43	50	59	60
NORTH DAKOTA								
Bismarck	47	29	18	10	14	26	44	42
Fargo	47	28	14	7	11	24	42	41
Williston	46	29	18	10	13	25	43	42
OHIO								
Cincinnati	60	46	37	36	37	44	56	57
Columbus	54	41	32	30	31	39	51	52
OKLAHOMA								
Oklahoma City	62	48	40	37	41	48	59	60

Table 6-1. (Continued)

CITIES	OCT.	NOV.	DEC.	JAN.	FEB.	MAR.	APR.	AVERAGE (12 MONTHS)
OREGON								
Astoria	53	46	43	41	43	45	49	51
Crater Lake	42	33	28	26	26	29	34	39
Portland	54	45	41	38	42	46	52	53
PENNSYLVANIA								
Philadelphia	56	44	34	32	33	41	52	54
Pittsburgh	53	41	31	29	29	37	49	50
SOUTH CAROLINA								
Charleston	66	56	50	50	52	57	65	65
SOUTH DAKOTA								
Rapid City	50	35	27	22	24	31	45	47
TENNESSEE								
Memphis	64	51	44	42	45	52	62	62
Nashville	62	49	41	40	42	49	60	60
TEXAS								
Amarillo	61	46	39	37	41	48	58	59
Brownsville	76	68	63	61	64	68	74	74
El Paso	64	51	44	43	49	55	63	63
Fort Worth	68	55	48	46	49	56	65	66
Houston	71	61	56	54	56	61	69	69
Midland	66	53	44	44	48	55	65	64
San Antonio	71	59	54	52	55	61	68	69
UTAH								
Salt Lake City	53	38	32	27	33	40	50	51
VERMONT								
Burlington	49	38	23	18	19	29	43	45
VIRGINIA								
Norfolk	62	51	43	41	42	48	58	60
WASHINGTON								
Seattle	52	44	41	38	41	44	49	51
Spokane	49	35	30	25	30	39	47	48
WISCONSIN								
Green Bay	49	34	22	17	18	28	43	44
WYOMING								
Lander	47	31	23	19	24	32	43	44
Yellowstone Park	42	29	22	18	22	27	38	40
PUERTO RICO								
San Juan	80	78	76	74	74	75	77	77

Climatic Atlas of the United States. U.S. Department of Commerce

where

Q = daily energy in Btu
G = gallons of water used per day
K = weight of water (8.34 lb/gal)
ΔT = difference between use temperature and supply temperature.

For this example

$$Q = 60 \times 8.34 \times (140 - 52.6)$$
$$= 43{,}735 \text{ Btu per day}$$

This is a monthly load of 1,355,785 Btu, and an annual load of 16,269,420 Btu. Since there are 3413 Btu/kWh, if the Grand Junction family paid a 3.36¢ per kWh electric bill, it would cost them $160 per year for hot water, using an electric heater that is 100% efficient.

$$\frac{16{,}269{,}420}{3413} \times 0.0336 = \$160$$

Table 6-2. Latitudes of Key Cities (degrees)

ALASKA			**INDIANA**	
Annette	55		Indianapolis	39
Barrow	71		**IOWA**	
Bethel	60		Ames	42
Fairbanks	64			
Matanuska	61		**KANSAS**	
			Dodge City	37
ARIZONA			Manhattan	39
Phoenix	33			
Tucson	32		**KENTUCKY**	
			Lexington	38
ARKANSAS				
Little Rock	34		**LOUISIANA**	
			Lake Charles	30
CALIFORNIA			New Orleans	30
Davis	38		Shreveport	32
Fresno	36			
Inyokern	35		**MAINE**	
Los Angeles	34		Caribou	46
Riverside	33		Portland	43
Santa Maria	34			
			MASSACHUSETTS	
COLORADO			Blue Hill	42
Boulder	40		Boston	42
Grand Junction	39		East Wareham	41
Grand Lake	40			
			MICHIGAN	
DISTRICT OF COLUMBIA	38		East Lansing	42
			Sault Ste. Marie	46
FLORIDA				
Apalachicola	29		**MINNESOTA**	
Gainsville	29		St. Cloud	45
Miami	25			
Tallahassee	30		**MISSOURI**	
Tampa	27		Columbia	38
GEORGIA			**MONTANA**	
Atlanta	33		Glasgow	48
Griffin	33		Great Falls	47
HAWAII			**NEBRASKA**	
Hilo	19		Lincoln	40
Honolulu	21		Omaha	41
IDAHO			**NEVADA**	
Boise	43		Ely	39
Twin Falls	42		Las Vegas	36
ILLINOIS			**NEW JERSEY**	
Chicago	41		Seabrook	39
Lemont	41			

Table 6-2. (Continued)

NEW MEXICO			RHODE ISLAND	
Albuquerque	35		Newport	41
NEW YORK			SOUTH CAROLINA	
Ithaca	42		Charleston	32
New York	40			
Sayville	40		SOUTH DAKOTA	
Schenectady	42		Rapid City	44
Upton	40			
			TENNESSEE	
NORTH CAROLINA			Nashville	36
Greensboro	36		Oak Ridge	36
Hatteras	35			
Raleigh/Durham	35		TEXAS	
			Brownsville	25
NORTH DAKOTA			El Paso	31
Bismarck	46		Fort Worth	32
			Midland	31
OHIO			San Antonio	29
Cleveland	41			
Columbus	40		UTAH	
			Salt Lake City	40
OKLAHOMA				
Oklahoma City	35		WASHINGTON	
Stillwater	36		Seattle	47
			Spokane	47
OREGON				
Astoria	46		WISCONSIN	
Corvallis	44		Madison	43
Medford	42			
			WYOMING	
PENNSYLVANIA			Lander	42
Pittsburgh	40		Laramie	41
State College	40			

Complete this calculation for your individual case, using the appropriate figures. It will give you an idea of what you might want to spend for a solar heater that would do the total job. If you have more specific information on what your actual hot water bill is (as did the homeowner in Chapter 1), don't rely on averages, use the actual figures.

If you want to pursue the economic analysis further, I will take you through some examples on sizing the system, following the procedure of Chapter 5. But again, recognize that they are approximations to help you put the claims of firms you may be considering in perspective.

CALCULATIONS OF COLLECTOR AREA

Remember the four factors we needed to calculate the area. These are:

- Load, in Btu
- Solar energy available
- Collector efficiency
- Percentage of load solar energy must supply

The load has just been calculated, so the next step is to determine the solar energy available. All the calculations will be made for Grand Junction. Looking at Table 1-4, we see that Grand Junction has an annual mean daily solar radiation of 456 langleys, or 1683 Btu/sq ft of horizontal surface (456 × 3.69 Btu/langley).

But collectors are not mounted horizontally. So what is the best angle to tilt them for year-round operation? Refer to the ASHRAE charts in Table 5-1, showing the total solar irradiation falling on inclined surfaces. Grand Junction is 39° north latitude (see Table 6-2 for latitude of key cities), so use the nearest equivalent, or 40°. Although the *demand* for hot water (60 gallons per day for this example) is fairly constant throughout the year, the *load* is greater during winter months, as the supply line temperature is lower. For best year-round performance, calculate the tilt angle favoring the heating season, October through April. Add the vertical surface total for the 21st day of each month during this period. Do the same for inclinations of L − 10°, L, L + 10°, and L + 20°. For 40°, these are:

COLLECTOR INCLINATION	TOTAL Btu/ft^2
Vertical (90°)	10,948
L − 10°	13,518
L	14,094
L + 10°	14,268
L + 20%	14,028

Looking at these totals, the maximum annual insolation is available wth an inclination of L + 10°, so the collector should be facing south and tilted at 49° for maximum year-round performance. To find the radiation multiplier, total the horizontal irradiation for each month and divide it into the annual L + 10° figure.

Table 6-3. Solar Energy Available in Grand Junction For an Average Month

Langley/day-ft^2	456
Btu/day-ft^2	1683
Latitude	39°
Collector angle	49°
Radiation multiplier	1.15
Collectable energy Btu/day-ft^2	1935
Collectable energy Btu/month-ft^2	59,985

COLLECTOR INCLINATION	ANNUAL TOTAL Btu/ft^2
Horizontal (0°)	21,326
L + 10°	24,574

The radiation multiplier equals 1.15. This tells us that tilting the collectors to 49° provides 15% more radiation than if they were horizontal. With this tilt, the previous calculation of 1683 Btu ft^2-day falling on a horizontal surface in Grand Junction should be increased by 15% to 1935. To summarize our data, see Table 6-3. For collector efficiency, assume that a double-pane, flat plate collector with a selective surface has been chosen (Table 6-4).

The collector efficiency may be read directly from Fig. 5-4. To calculate the collector area for 100% solar dependency during an average month, multiply the monthly collectable energy (in Btu) by the collector efficiency, and divide this figure into the monthly energy used (in Btu).

$$A = \frac{1,355,785}{59,985 \times 0.54} = 42 \text{ sq ft}$$

If you want 100% solar dependency during the "worst" month (which is December for Grand Junction), refer to Table 6-5. Also, you must consider that, since the average outdoor

Table 6-4. Calculation of Collector Efficiency

Average absorber temperature	150°F
Daily average outdoor temperature (annual)	53°F
Temperature difference (ΔT)	97°F
Collector efficiency	54%

Table 6-5. Solar Energy Available in Grand Junction in December

Langley/day-ft^2	212
Btu/day-ft^2	782
Radiation multiplier	2.2
Collectable energy Btu/day-ft^2	1720
Collectable energy Btu/month-ft^2	53,320

temperature during December is 29°F, the load on the heater increases while the efficiency of the collectors decreases. The load becomes:

$$Q = 1,721,876 \text{ Btu/month}$$

With a collector efficiency of 10%, the required collector area is:

$$A = \frac{1,721,876}{53,320 \times 0.5} = 65 \text{ sq ft}$$

What is the best collector size to use? To answer this question, an economic analysis of the system is required. Start the calculation using a collector area designed to provide 100% service for the "average" month and work down from there. Rarely is it profitable to size for the "worst" month, as more energy is collected than needed during most of the year.

ECONOMIC ANALYSIS OF SYSTEM

A chart similar to that used in Chapter 5 (for a room heating system) should be prepared. Table 6-6 shows an example analysis chart, using Grand Junction, Colorado as an example. The latitude is 39°, with the collector inclined at 49° (L + 10°), assuming a collector efficiency of 54% each month. Notice that I have made calculations for a 42 sq ft system needed to supply 100% of the hot water load on an "average" month, and also on a 20 sq ft system, so we can compare the economics. You should note that more energy is being produced by the 42 sq ft system in the months of May through October than is required. This is wasted heat in an economic sense as shown in Table 6-7. If you have selected a system selling for $20 per sq ft installed, a 20 sq ft size would cost $400, saving you $76 a year. At this rate, it would take 5.3 years to pay off. For a 42 sq ft size, the payoff would be 6 years at a fixed electric rate of 3.36¢ per kWh. The obvious choice is the

Table 6-6. Economical Analysis of a Sample System

Month	Insolation (Btu/day-ft²)	Radiation Multiplier	Collectable energy (Btu/month-ft²×1000)	Energy required (Btu/month×1000)	Energy collected by 20 sq ft system (Btu/month×1000)	Percentage of energy supplied by 20 sq ft system	Energy collected by 42 sq ft system (Btu/month×1000)	Percentage of energy supplied by 42 sq ft system
January	837	2.0	52	1768	562	32	1180	67
February	1195	1.6	59	1660	637	38	1339	81
March	1600	1.2	59	1520	637	42	1339	88
April	2013	0.9	54	1321	583	44	1226	93
May	2268	0.8	56	1210	605	50	1271	105
June	2610	0.8	63	1036	680	66	1430	138
July	2492	0.8	62	962	670	70	1407	146
August	2194	0.9	61	993	659	66	1385	139
September	1895	1.2	68	1081	734	68	1544	143
October	1375	1.6	68	1319	734	56	1544	117
November	959	2.0	58	1516	626	41	1317	87
December	782	2.2	53	1722	572	33	1203	70

larger system. Just as a matter of interest, however, if you had decided to use a collector area of 65 sq ft to provide 100% solar energy service during December, the system cost of $1300 would take 8 years to pay off. You can see in Table 6-8 that the payoff moves up slightly to just over five years at an 8% annual fuel-use escalation. Even without fuel increases, this 42 sq ft water heating system is a good investment for the Grand Junction family—again provided that the unit will

Table 6-7. Comparing Systems

Month	Energy required (Btu/month×1000)	Energy collected by 20 sq ft system (Btu/month×1000)	Energy collected by 42 sq ft system (Btu/month×1000)	Monthly kWh saved (20 sq ft system)	Monthly kWh saved (42 sq ft system)	Dollar savings of 3.36¢kWh)	
						20 sq ft system	42 sq ft system
January	1768	562	1180	165	346	6	12
February	1660	637	1339	187	392	6	13
March	1520	637	1339	187	392	6	13
April	1321	583	1226	171	359	6	12
May	1210	605	1271	177	354	6	12
June	1036	680	1430	199	304	7	10
July	962	670	1407	196	282	7	9
August	993	659	1385	193	291	6	10
September	1081	734	1544	215	317	7	11
October	1319	734	1544	215	386	7	13
November	1516	626	1317	183	386	6	13
December	1722	572	1203	168	352	6	12
Annual totals	16,108	7699	16,185	2256	4161	76	140

Table 6-8. Fuel Cost Increasing at 8% Compounded Annually

Year	Fuel Cost (¢kWh)	Yearly Savings ($)	Cumulative Savings ($)
1 (1975)	3.36	140	140
2	3.63	151	291
3	3.92	163	454
4	4.23	176	630
5	4.57	190	820
6	4.94	206	1026
7	5.33	222	1248
8	5.76	240	1488

perform as warranted and require minimum maintenance over a six-year period.

SIZING THE STORAGE TANK

Determining the exact combination of collector size and storage-tank capacity that results in maximum efficiency for each geographic location, family size, use pattern, and energy cost is an extremely complex problem that is best left to professional engineers. I can, however, offer some sound guidelines for purposes of comparison.

Following the same reasoning used in Chapter 5, you should consider a tank that will store enough energy to provide hot water over a period of two sunless days. For the Grand Junction family of three, their daily hot water requirements were calculated to be 43,735 Btu. For two days, 87,470 Btu are needed. The tank volume formula is the same as that used in Chapter 5:

$$V = \frac{E_s}{C_w \times \Delta T}$$

where

$E_s = 87{,}470$ Btu of energy stored
$C_w = 62.4$ Btu/ft^3-°F for water
$\Delta T = 140 - 52.6 = 87$°F

Here, the temperature difference (ΔT) is the same used to calculate the load or the use temperature (140°F) less the supply temperature (52.6). You will recall that the supply temperature was taken as the annual average daily temperature for Grand Junction Colorado.

$$V = \frac{87,470}{62.4 \times 87}$$
$$= 16 \text{ cu ft}$$
$$= 121 \text{ gallons of water}$$

If the storage tank is connected in series with a conventional water heater, as pictured in Fig. 6-6, there is no need to store this quantity of water, as a guaranteed supply of hot water can be provided by the conventional unit. In this case, consider a supplementary storage tank for a one-day supply with a volume:

$$V = \frac{43,735}{62.4 \times 87}$$

$$= 8 \text{ cu ft}$$
$$= 60 \text{ gallons of water}$$

SUMMARY

Those of you who have adequate sunshine and are presently operating your water heaters on electricity will probably see an advantage to investing in a solar energy unit. A switch to solar energy from natural gas at present prices is not so promising, but gas prices are expected to rise rapidly as federal price controls are relaxed. Those homes in more remote locations where "bottled" gas is used may be a little closer to solar conversion.

You now have enough background to explore various combinations of solar collector materials that would provide improved efficiency. For example: one cover pane or two on the collectors? Selective surface on the absorbers or flat-black paint? Will the extra cost be offset by the efficiency? Remember, what you want to know, in the final analysis, is—what does the system cost per Btu of usable heat collected?

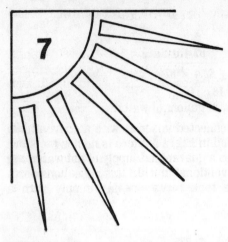

7

Heating a Swimming Pool With Solar Energy

It may be argued that using precious natural gas to heat swimming pools is an improper allocation of natural resources. Until recently there appeared to be an adequate supply of gas for industrial uses, new residential construction, and swimming pools. With today's reappraisal of the quantity of our natural resources, however, some of our larger states have banned the use of natural gas for pool heating, which they consider a "luxury." New York, Illinois, and California are among those refusing to hook up any new gas-fired pool heaters.

Heating pools by solar energy can provide an acceptable alternative. As with other solar applications, you cannot rely on the sun to heat your pool at a specific time, nor to the particular temperature you may require. The sun is temperamental; it does not always shine. And your "storage tank" is the pool itself, which loses heat at night and on cloudy days. The best you can expect from a solar-heated pool installation is to extend your pool season, raise the temperature of the pool water by 10°F, and provide a net dollar savings after the solar installation reaches its payback period. If your family enjoys swimming beyond the normal pool season (mid-June through mid-September), and if you are concerned about the cost and availability of fuels and have adequate sunshine, then by all means you should consider a solar heater.

Just as I recommended insulating your house before "solarizing" it, a pool cover may make ecomomic sense, especially if you live in an area with cold, clear nights and relatively low humidity. Generally speaking, a pool in the sun will gain 2° to 3°F of its temperature during the day from the sunshine falling on its surface and will store this energy until it reaches a temperature 10°F higher than the outside or ambient air temperature. At this point it reaches an equilibrium, losing heat at night equal to the net gain during the day; all you can expect without a cover, solar panels, or supplementary heat is pool water 10°F above the average air temperature.

A plastic pool cover should provide an additional 10°F gain. Now you are at 20°F above the outside air, but most people prefer to swim in water heated to 80° to 82°F, and this requires some supplementary heat. This can be a solar heating system working alone, or with a conventional gas-fired heater if fuel is available.

POOL COVERS

Devices advertised as pool covers vary from round discs designed to look like floating "lily pads" to plastic "ping-pong" balls, which float on the pool surface covering as much area as possible. Both of these concepts make some energy-saving contribution. But I would doubt their cost effectiveness, and certainly it is troublesome to remove and replace them before and after each swim session.

Most pool owners prefer the more conventional covers made with a continuous piece of transparent plastic-sheeting material. The efficiency of this type of cover is higher if the plastic is floating on the surface of the pool water, with as few air bubbles between the sheet and water as possible. If air bubbles are present, water will condense, forming droplets that act as reflectors of solar energy and minimize the heat gain. The primary purpose of the plastic cover is to reduce the heat losses from the pool and, just like other forms of "insulation," its use becomes more critical as the difference between the pool temperature and outside air temperature increases.

SOLAR PANELS

A typical solar panel installation, shown in Fig. 7-1, presents an effective method for providing economical pool heat. For swimming pool applications, panels are generally

Fig. 7-1. A typical solar panel installation using solar energy to heat a swimming pool. (Courtesy Raypak, Inc., Westlake Village, Calif.)

constructed from plastic, rubber, or metal, in that order. There are literally thousands of plastic and rubber formulations available, and most of them are unsuitable for solar panel use. Proper inhibitors must be used to prevent the ultraviolet rays of the sun from degrading plastic and to prevent ozone from cracking rubber components. Also, some types of plastic, such as polyolefin, tend to *potato chip* or *curl* after repeated heating and cooling cycles.

Each manufacturer will claim his product is made of the correct material, and most homeowners do not have the technical information required to evaluate these claims. The best advice I can give you, in the absence of federal test standards, is to know the company with whom you are dealing, including its business history, reputation, and warranty policy.

If you are considering a metal panel, be sure to thoroughly investigate the possibility of corrosion. Swimming pool water should never be circulated directly through aluminum absorbers, because accelerated corrosion can cause early failure. Most designs use copper tubes covered with aluminum pictured in Fig. 7-2. The swimming pool water would not be a hazard to the aluminum in this case. The aluminum is used to capture heat economically and transfer it through the copper to the pool water.

Plastic panels are marketed in several shapes. One resembles a window shade. It is 48 in. wide and available in 8 or 10 ft lengths. The concept is shown in Fig. 7-3. If you examine the cross section (A—A), you can see the small water passages extruded into the polyolefin plastic absorber, which is adhesively bonded to 2⅜ in. plastic headers. The individual panels are connected to form a module with sufficient square footage to heat the pool to the desired temperature. Panels are attached to the roof structure, using nylon straps in a manner similar to that shown in Fig. 7-4. It is a good idea to remove the panels from the roof if a hurricane, or similar heavy weather conditions, is known to be advancing.

One metal panel presently marketed uses all-copper water passages with an aluminum filler sheet painted black to improve efficiency. If you refer to Fig. 7-2, you will see that the ⅜ in. diameter copper waterways are spaced and soldered to 1½ in. diameter copper headers. This assembly is then covered with 0.02 in. thick aluminum sheet, painted black and riveted in place. Figure 7-5 shows the completed panel

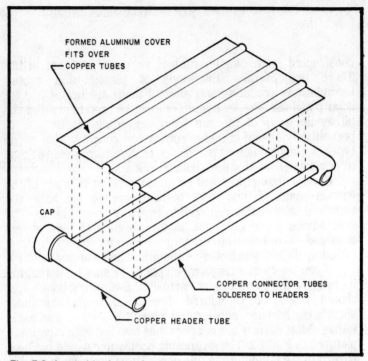

Fig. 7-2. A suitable design for a metal solar panel for a swimming pool. Copper is used in contact with the pool water; aluminum captures the heat economically.

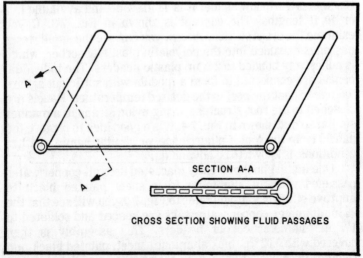

SECTION A-A

CROSS SECTION SHOWING FLUID PASSAGES

Fig. 7-3. A commonly used plastic panel with extruded water passages.

mounted on a wooden subframe, which is then attached to the roof rafters with lag screws.

There is the possibility of galvanic corrosion on bimetallic systems where copper and aluminum are in contact with each other. This can occur if moisture is present to act as an electrolyte (or conductor), where you have all the conditions necessary to form a "battery." The secret is to keep moisture from collecting next to the copper and aluminum joint. Silicon sealers or points are frequently used for this purpose.

You may have noted that I have called these assemblies "panels" instead of "solar collectors." The reason is that, generally, no cover panes or insulation is needed, leaving just an absorber *panel*. If you refer to the efficiency curve in Fig. 5-4, note that as the temperature difference (ΔT) becomes

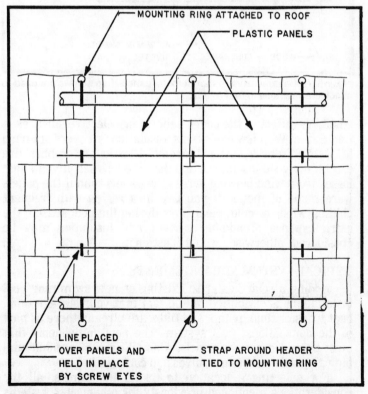

Fig. 7-4. One method of attaching plastic panels (of the type shown in Figure 7-3) to a roof structure.

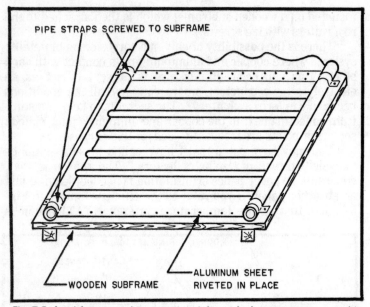

PIPE STRAPS SCREWED TO SUBFRAME

ALUMINUM SHEET
RIVETED IN PLACE

WOODEN SUBFRAME

Fig. 7-5. A subframe used to mount metal panels. Lag screws are used to
attach the subframe to roof rafters.

small, the effect of the cover pane(s) or selective surfaces is
minimized. With few exceptions, insulation or covers are hard
to justify from a cost standpoint. Plastic and rubber are
essentially good insulators, and they are less sensitive to heat
losses from wind blowing across the panels than if the panels
were made of metal. If you live in a region with frequent
chilling winds or cold, clear days during the pool season, the
extra expense of adding a cover and insulation may be
considered; otherwise I would question it.

TYPICAL SYSTEM ARRANGEMENTS

Adding a solar heater to existing or new swimming pool
installations is simplified by the fact that your storage tank,
heat transfer fluid, pump, and filter are already there as part
of the conventional pool system. The new components that
must be added are the panels, a small amount of additional
piping, and the necessary valves and controls.

For selecting a location to install the panels, all the
considerations mentioned previously for other solar systems
would apply. Of course, they should be located as close to the

pool's pumping and recirculation system as possible to keep additional plumbing lines short. Also, the mounting angle will change from the "latitude plus 10°" recommended for winter heating. I will give you more specifics on this later in this chapter.

Manual System

The simplest system is a *manual* one, which may be used with or without an auxiliary pool heater. Referring to Fig. 7-6, water from the pool is diverted through the solar panels when gate valve V_2 is closed. Note that check valve V_1 is installed at the outlet of the filter. This is necessary to prevent any water that is drained from the solar system from "backwashing" the filter. The float-type air vent valve V_3 allows air to escape from the solar panel lines when water first flows into them, and allows air to enter the line when the panels are being drained. This valve should be installed at the highest point in the system. If you have, or plan to use, an auxiliary heater, this manually operated solar unit may be hooked in series with it, instead of the automatic controls of Fig. 7-7.

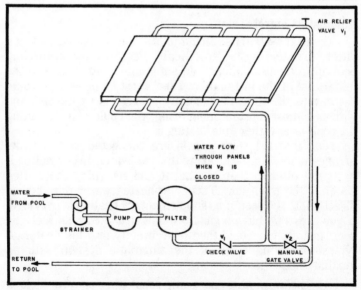

Fig. 7-6. A solar heating system with manual controls used for a swimming pool.

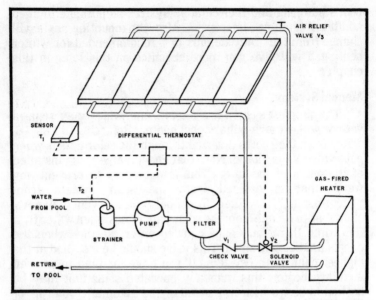

Fig. 7-7. A solar pool heater with automatic controls and an auxiliary gas-fired heater.

Automatic Control System

The next system has an *automatic* control system, using a differential thermostat specifically designed for swimming pool applications. Although an automatic control adds to the initial cost of the installation, I feel most homeowners would not devote the time to manually operate the controls. And without almost constant monitoring, you could end up cooling the pool water rather than heating it.

Note that the solar panels are connected in a parallel arrangement (Fig. 7-7), taking the pool water directly after it has been filtered, then heating it and returning the heated water to the main line. This solar-heated water may be fed directly into the pool, if no supplementary heating is provided. If you presently have a gas-fired heater and can get fuel, the solar installation would then feed directly into the heater. A typical operating cycle of the automatic system with an auxiliary heater is:

1) The swimming pool pump runs either on a time clock or continuously, as preferred. The pump operation is completely independent of solar panel controls.

2) Sensor T_1 is basically a miniature solar panel. When a thermostat attached to the panel reads a temperature 5°F higher than the pool water, solenoid valve V_2 is closed, forcing the pool water through the solar panels.

3) Sensor T_2 monitors the pool water temperature and opens valve V_2 when the temperature difference (ΔT) is 2°F. That is, when the sensor T_1 is only 2°F hotter than the pool water, the solar panels are bypassed, and the pool water is sent directly into the gas heater.

4) The gas heater has its own individual thermostat, and it will operate if the water temperature entering the unit is below the thermostatic setting.

5) When the pool pump is stopped, float-type air vent valve V_3 opens, allowing air to enter the line and draining the water from the panels and distribution piping. V_2 remains open when the pump is stopped.

It is important to remember that solar swimming pool panels have different operating conditions than collectors for water heaters or room heating. The swimming pool (which is your storage tank) has a very large volume. A small quantity of high-temperature water flowing slowly in the pool would make only a small contribution to the overall temperature of the water in the pool. Remember, your objective is to raise the temperature only 10°F; a rapid flow of pool water through the panels does this most efficiently. Refer to the efficiency curve of Fig. 5-4 and you can see how it pays to keep the water flowing rapidly and the temperature difference small. Plastic collectors should be cool to the touch, with pool water flowing through them at the proper rate. To keep the flow rate high, be sure the pump is of adequate size and that the panels have a low pressure drop (or minimum restriction to the flow of water). Insufficient flow may also be caused by a dirty filter or piping that is too small in diameter.

Self-draining of the panels is an important feature to prevent freezing, as well as overheating if the pump becomes inoperative on hot days. Water in the panels can freeze at night, even with air temperatures above 32°F, due to radiation losses. Water expands as it freezes and will most assuredly burst pipes, rupture panels, and ruin your system unless protection is provided. Check for these features on any system you are considering.

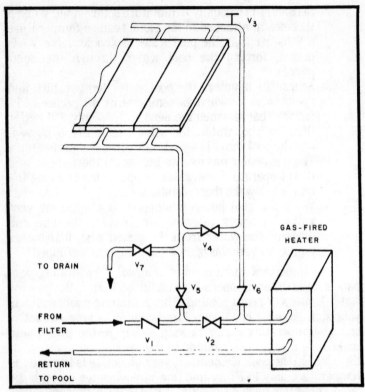

Fig. 7-8. A plumbing diagram showing optional bypass, isolation, and drain valves.

Bypass Systems

Some systems use a bypass in the collector line (Fig. 7-8). Although it adds a little to the expense, the extra valves and bypass shown are worth your consideration. The bypass valve (V_4) is manually operated, and allows you to reduce the pressure drop across the solar panels by allowing some of the pool water to "bypass" them. Water will flow through the most direct path. If V_4 is fully open, the solar panels would make little, if any, heat contribution, since most of the pool water would flow through V_4. The bypass also helps in draining water from the return piping. Manual gate valve V_5 and check valve V_6 serve to completely isolate the solar system and, if repairs are needed, they can be operated without shutting down the pool pump. Valve V_7 is a hand-operated drain valve, which can be used to completely drain the panels and lines when it and the bypass valve are open and gate valve V₅ is closed.

APPROXIMATING PANEL SIZE AND ORIENTATION

In virtually all solar-product literature concerned with heating swimming pools, the suggested square footage of panels is related to the surface area of the pool—not to its volume. For an approximation, this approach may be suitable; the pool itself is fairly well insulated against heat loss, with the exception of its surface. The big job is to raise the pool temperature to 80°F initially, and here the volume is a factor. Once the pool water reaches 80°F, all the solar unit must do is gain enough heat during the day to compensate for losses at night. The question here is how quickly do you want the system to respond? Let's assume your pool is 18 by 36 ft and holds 22,000 gallons of water. As there are 7.48 gallons in each cubic foot, this converts to 2941 cu ft. It takes 62.4 Btu to raise one cubic foot of water 1°F; increasing the temperature of the pool in this example by 10°F requires 1,835,184 Btu. Where will this energy come from, and how soon?

No one can predict the weather with 100% accuracy, but what I would like to develop for you is a method for approximating a reasonable panel size for your area and an ideal orientation and inclination of these panels. The big unknown, aside from the number of continuous sunny days you might have, will be panel efficiency. Unfortunately, in the absence of national standards, you will be somewhat at the mercy of manufacturers' claims, and individual designs and flow rates. To bring this into perspective, I will assume that a maximum efficiency of 70% can be achieved by a well-designed unit.

The ideal panel orientation is facing due south. For a determination of the optimum mounting angle, refer to the

Table 7-1. Daily Solar Energy Available in Grand Junciton During the Month of May

Langley/day-ft²	615
Btu/day-ft²	2268
Latitude	39°
Panel angle	29°
Radiation multiplier	1.01
Collectable energy Btu/day-ft²	2291

ASHRAE tables in Table 5-1, showing total solar irradiation for different latitudes and inclinations. Assume the pool season is May through September and the latitude of your location is 40°. Add the L − 10°, L, L + 10°, and horizontal surface figures for the months in question. For 40°, they are:

INCLINATION	TOTAL Btu/ft^2
Horizontal	11,766
L − 10°	11,849
L	11,204
L + 10°	10,306

In theory, the best inclination for 40° latitudes is L − 10° for the season being studied, and this will be used for this example. In practice, the slope of the existing roof generally determines the inclination.

You can make your own calculation as to what penalty in performance would result from other slopes. Remember that you need to provide drainage and an even flow of water through the panels. Slopes less than 5° are not practical. Even this may vary with the specific panel chosen. Note that our radiation multiplier here is 1.01 (11,849 divided by 11,766).

Assume the pool for which we are making these calculations is in Grand Junction, Colorado. From the mean daily solar radiation figures in Table 5-1, a calculation of the solar energy available at the start of the pool season should be made.

If you use the pool industry's rule of thumb, that a panel area equal to 50% of the pool surface should be used, for the 18 by 36 ft size pool this equals 324 sq ft of panel. At 70% efficiency, each square foot of panel surface could theoretically provide 1604 Btu per day (2291 × 0.7), or 324 sq ft supplying 519,695 Btu/day. At this rate, it would take 3½ sunny days to raise the pool temperature 10°F. Remember that the sun is also helping to heat the pool directly, by shining on its surface. Once the pool is up to the required temperature, all the solar panels must do is balance the nighttime losses; you would not need to wait another 3½ days for the temperature to build up, unless a period of cloudy weather developed.

ECONOMICS OF A SOLAR POOL HEATER

I have seen ads for solar pool heaters that are generally misleading. Statements boasting proven pool heating systems

Table 7-2. Calculating the Equivalent Cost of Gas

Month	Btu/month-ft^2 available ($\times$1000)	Btu/month Collected By 324 sq ft of panels ($\times$1000)	Equivalent cost of gas (at 18¢/therm)
May	71	16,111	$ 29
June	79	17,917	32
July	78	17,690	32
August	69	15,649	28
Sept.	57	12,928	23
		Total for the season:	$144

that let you heat your pool without cost should make you wary. The sunshine may be free, but certainly not the system, installation, and maintenance. I suggest you perform a thorough economic analysis and reach your own conclusion.

Staying with the Grand Junction example, for the 18 by 36 ft. pool, it was determined that 324 sq ft of panel can theoretically supply 519,695 Btu on a sunny day in May. If the sun shines every day and all the energy collected could be used, the May total of 16,110,545 Btu would offset an equivalent amount of heat energy from burning natural gas. At a cost of 18¢/therm (a therm is 100,000 Btu), this would present a savings of $29 for the month. Extend this calculation through the pool season of May through September, using Table 7-2.

Assuming that the system, including 324 sq ft of panels, costs $1440 installed and was 70% efficient, and that you could use all the energy collected during the swimming season, it would take ten years to pay back at a gas cost of 18¢/therm. If the cost of gas doubles, the payback period is five years. This is a rough calculation with lots of assumptions and no allowances for maintenence. But it does give you a method for approximating the realized value of the unit. With the expected rise in gas rates, if gas is available at all, it may be just a question of time until solar pool heat is your only option.

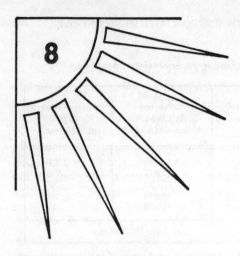

8

Precautions and Advice for Consumers

As the solar industry is relatively new, there has been insufficient time to develop a set of national standards, uniform building codes, long-term performance data, and business history. The homeowner investing in an expensive solar system must have some assurances that (1) the economics truly justify the installation, that (2) building codes will be satisfied and that (3) the system will be properly installed and function with minimum maintenance during its design life. To have reasonable confidence in the investment at this stage assumes the homeowner has one or more of the following:

- Absolute trust in the manufacturer's literature and the installer's techniques.
- Legal safeguards to provide repair, replacement, or refund, as appropriate.
- Assistance from registered professional architects, engineers, or attorneys.

To act on the first point alone is a dangerous approach, since the majority of firms selling solar equipment today are new enterprises, and you may not be familiar with their product or business history. That "nice, sincere sounding salesman" may be working for another company tomorrow, so I would strongly encourage you to look for protection of your investment, and this chapter provides additional thoughts for your consideration.

ASSURANCE THAT THE PRODUCT WILL WORK

There are very few companies today that offer a complete solar "system." Water heaters may be an exception, but even here, one company will not be producing all the components used in its system. On the other hand, component manufacturers abound, having collectors, heat exchangers, motors, valves, storage tanks, and controls readily available. Each reputable component manufacturer believes in his individual product, and most manufacturers will guarantee their product to be free from defects in materials and workmanship. They refrain, however, from guaranteeing performance of a "system" which they do not produce, and this is understandable.

An example of this is shown in the sales literature of a typical major solar collector manufacturer:

> The _____ solar collector is intended for installation and/or use by persons having the requisite skill and know-how at their own discretion and risk. Thus _____ makes no warranties or representations regarding the performance of the_____ solar collector and takes no responsibility for its installation, for the system designs, or for any matters directly or indirectly relating thereto or arising therefrom.

The homeowner is interested in what the *system* will do—not any of its individual components; and the person selling that system should be prepared to guarantee its performance under a specific set of conditions. No one can guarantee what the weather will be, but the system must be sold using long-term historical weather data for your specific region, not some "ideal" conditions simulated in a laboratory or taken at noon in the middle of the desert. Similarly, a high-quality aluminum absorber can be ruined in a few months if connected directly to copper plumbing circulating a conductive fluid. Is this kind of failure the responsibility of the manufacturer of the absorber, collector, or copper plumbing? Definitely not, unless they sold the system or guaranteed performance under these conditions. You must look to the system seller for protection. He, in turn, will seek adjustments from his component suppliers commensurate with their warranties.

Eventually, the National Bureau of Standards will establish performance criteria for solar heating/cooling systems which, if met, can be used by the FHA, banks, savings and loan companies, and others as a basis for lending money to purchase and install a solar heating system. There are many qualified groups working diligently with the National Bureau of Standards (NBS) on these performance criteria. They include the American Society of Heating, Refrigeration, and Air Conditioning Engineers (ASHRAE), the American National Standards Institute (ANSI), the American Society for Testing Materials (ASTM), and others. Interim standards are available, and they may be obtained by writing to the Government Printing Office, Washington, D.C. 20402. Ask for the booklet entitled *Interim Performance Criteria for Solar Heating and Combined Heating/Cooling Systems and Dwellings* (stock number 0324-01043). Several independent test laboratories throughout the nation will be certified to test systems according to NBS standards. I suggest your system's supplier have such certified test data available.

It would be a good idea to ask the firm that is selling your system what other solar jobs they have done in your area, both public and private. You should try to see one in operation and review the actual performance data.

COMPLIANCE WITH REGULATIONS AND STANDARDS

Aside from the work of the National Bureau of Standards, you should check with your local building department. When a new building system is available, the general procedure is for the manufacturer to obtain an interim approval from national code bodies, such as the International Congress of Building Organizations. (ICBO). Bulletins announcing these approvals are circulated to thousands of local building departments, which generally do not have the time nor the budgets to check out each and every system.

Certainly there may be local restrictions or ordinances that override national approvals, and this is for your local building inspector to decide. If the system is approved, the building inspector will issue a certificate so stating. Such a certificate does not mean the department endorses the system, merely that the system meets local code regulations. Once you have decided on a system and its installer, give the department a call to ask if a certification is on file. They may also be able to tell you about any building permits they have issued for similar systems. It would be helpful to talk to other homeowners who have the product and get their reactions. Your system salesman will readily provide the names of happy customers, but disappointed ones are hard to come by.

There are other sources you can ask to help distinguish quality systems from inferior ones. The Solar Energy Industries Association (SEIA), 1001 Connecticut Avenue, N.W., Washington, D.C. 20036 has an ethics committee to encourage its members to fulfill all contractual obligations and, if a warranty is given, to perform promptly on such warranty where justifiable claims are in order. In addition, SEIA hopes to provide the public with clearly explained economic considerations of its solar energy equipment purchases. Also, there is the Office of Consumer Affairs, Department of Health, Education, and Welfare, Washington, D.C. that has published a booklet on this subject for consumers. Information may be obtained by writing to Joseph C. Dawson, Public Affairs Director.

WHO WILL INSTALL THE SYSTEM?

For homeowner satisfaction, there can be no "weak links in the chain," starting with well-designed, compatible components engineered into a system that is correctly installed to provide maximum operating efficiency with a minimum of maintenance. Hopefully, manufacturers will establish high standards in the selection of dealers, installers, and service personnel, providing them with seminars and training sessions to do their jobs correctly.

Some of the areas that should be checked during installation are:

- Proper grounding of the electrical system.
- Sufficient valves to isolate components.
- Freedom from fluid leaks.
- No loose wires or loose sensor attachments.
- Correct orientation and inclination of collectors.
- Proper pump capacity.
- Freedom from shade on collectors.
- Adequate size pipes.
- Balanced flow.
- Sufficient collector and plumbing line insulation.
- No air entrapment in lines or collectors.
- Collectors properly secured to structure.

When making your arrangements, be sure the installed price of the system includes all the details. Items that are frequently overlooked are glazing, sheet-metal work, complete electrical and plumbing services and, occasionally, the building permit itself. Needless to say, contractors should be licensed, have adequate insurance, and escrow or bond any deposits given to them until the job is complete.

Quick calls to the Better Business Bureau, the Chamber of Commerce, and The Association of General Contractors can provide additional information on the firms with whom you plan to deal.

LEGAL CONSIDERATIONS

The subjects mentioned in this section may not present problems, either to you individually or to your community. They have nonetheless, been discussed at many solar conferences, and define questions that must be resolved before the use of solar energy obtains widespread acceptance.

First, there is the regulation of building materials and design. This can be accomplished by either prescriptive standards or performance criteria. Generally, building officials resist changes until performance of a product or system is proven according to accepted standards. It is this question of standards that is being worked on so diligently now under the direction of NBS, but this will take time to develop. Model building codes covering solar systems are being developed by the Building Research Advisory Board (BRAB) of the National Academy of Sciences, Washington, D.C. Some cities with critical needs have proceeded on their own to develop codes. One such community, Colorado Springs, Colorado, faced with the curtailment of natural gas, developed a code which includes the following points:

- ASHRAE method for load calculation.
- Provision for 100% backup system.
- Use of solar component data published in NBS 74-634 and 635.
- Provision for winds and snow loads.
- Collector materials capable of withstanding 400°F temperatures.
- Fire dampers in air collector ducts.
- Noncombustible and nonoutgassing insulation.
- Provisions against freezing.
- Minimum thickness of ⅛ in. for tempered glass covers.
- Noncorrosive and nonelectrolytic heat transfer fluids.
- Provisions for expansion and contraction.
- Safeguards against rupture, leakage, and contamination.

Information on the complete building code for Colorado Springs may be obtained by contacting the city officials.

Another legal question, one of *sun rights*, must ultimately be resolved. The right to light has been disputed for many years, going back in English common law to the "Law of Ancient Lights," which still exists in Great Britain. Today in that country, if light has been received for a minimum 27-year period, it cannot be blocked by a neighboring structure beyond a point defined as the *grumble line*. Definitions are difficult, but the British have attempted to define this location.

No such law exists in the United States and, although there seems to be little question that we are entitled to receive all light coming directly over our property, light coming across perimeter boundaries is not protected by law. Casting a shadow is not against the law. Since solar collectors do not function well in the shade, how do we insure against a high-rise structure or a neighbor's growing tree blocking our sunshine?

One possible solution is to buy an "easement to light," which transfers with the property title just as a conventional easement does. Insofar as trees are concerned, Colorado Springs has a "tree control bill" pending, to minimize the impact of increased tree height on collectors. Additional options would relate to zoning laws, which govern setback and structure-height limits. On large-scale developments, such as subdivisions and shopping centers, it would be possible to mandate solar easements through zoning. I am sure you will see responsible communities offering short-term solutions to this "sun rights" question. Long-term legal solutions must follow if the use of solar energy becomes widespread.

If you are planning to build a new home, incorporating solar heating or cooling, try to pick an architectural/ engineering firm that has sound experience in solar energy design. Look around for one having completed projects with operating data on the solar equipment for you to review.

Most professional architects or engineers do not have an interest in the manufacture or sale of a solar system, so there is no conflict. They perform analyses of sites (including weather surveys), calculate heating demands and heating yields, and can "optimize" the design of a solar system for you. Good professional advice is a must for those larger projects, which frequently have a solar "budget" of 10% of the total cost of the dwelling.

Appendix A
Glossary

When you begin to shop for a solar-powered system to suit your needs, whether it be for room or space heating, water heating, swimming pool heating, or any combination of these, you will undoubtedly come up against terminology with which you will find yourself unfamiliar. This is inevitable, for as new technological advances come about, new words, or old words with a new meaning, must be used to accommodate those advances. The following list of terms will help put you on an equal footing with salesmen and literature dealing with solar energy systems.

absorptance—The ratio of the amount of radiation absorbed by a surface to the amount of radiation falling upon it.

absorptivity—The capacity of a material to absorb radiant energy.

ambient temperature—The temperature of the surrounding atmosphere. When discussing solar collectors, this term refers to the outside air temperature in the location of the collectors.

auxiliary heating system—Equipment utilizing conventional energy sources to supplement the output provided by the solar system.

backwashing—A term describing the reverse flow of water through a swimming pool filter; also known as *backflow*. Backflow may be prevented through the use of check valves.

British thermal unit—The amount of energy required to increase the temperature of 1 pound of water by 1° Fahrenheit, abbreviated Btu.

check valve—A valve that allows fluid to flow in one direction only. It may also be called a *backflow preventer*.

components—The various elements that make a solar system, such as valves, controls, pumps, etc.

conduction—The transfer of heat through or between bodies in contact in the absence of fluid motion.

conductor—A substance through which electricity or heat can flow readily.

convection—The transfer of heat due to the motion of a liquid or gas.

cooling degree day—The number of degrees that the daily mean temperature is above 65°F.

degree day—The number of degrees that the daily mean temperature varies from 65°F. See *heating degree day* and *cooling degree day*.

delta T—The temperature differential between two points, symbolized as ΔT.

design life—The period of time during which a system is expected to perform its intended function without requiring major maintenance or replacement.

dielectric fitting—An insulating or nonconducting fitting used to isolate different metals. See *galvanic corrosion*.

diffuse radiation—Radiant solar energy that is widely scattered, such as that present on a hazy day.

emittance—The ratio of the radiant energy emitted (or given off) by a surface to the energy emitted by a surface considered to have almost perfect absorptance (called a *black body*) when the surfaces are at the same temperature.

galvanic corrosion—The decay or corrosion of dissimilar metals caused by an electric current flowing between them through an electrolyte. The rate of corrosion is a function of the metals involved.

glazing—Setting glass or other transparent cover materials into the frames of solar collectors. Dual glazing refers to the application of two cover panes.

header—A section of pipe or internal fluid passage that carries the main body of heat transfer fluid at the top and bottom of some solar absorber panels. Headers are used to connect the smaller perpendicular fluid channels.

heat capacity—The amount of heat necessary to raise the temperature of a given mass one degree Fahrenheit.

heating degree day—The number of degrees that the daily mean temperature is below 65°F.

heat transfer medium—A fluid (either liquid or air) used to transport thermal energy.

infrared—Invisible light rays just beyond the visible spectrum. Also called *long-wave radiation.*

insolation—The radiation of the sun received by a surface. The rate of such radiation per unit of surface is measured in langleys or Btu.

kilowatt-hour—A unit of electrical power equal to 1000 watts. Abbreviated kWh.

langley—A measure of the total solar radiation, both direct and diffuse, falling on a horizontal surface (1 langley/day = 3.687 Btu/ft^2 -day).

outgassing—The process by which materials and components expel gas.

payback period—The period of time necessary to recapture an initial expenditure, once operating and maintenance costs have been considered.

pitting—The process through which localized wear is caused in materials by erosion from heat transfer fluids or chemical decomposition.

radiation—The transfer of energy through space or matter by means other than conduction or convection.

retrofit—Installation of a solar system in an existing structure.

selective coating—One having high absorptivity for incoming solar radiation and low emittance.

sensors—Devices used to measure or sense individual parameters, such as temperature, flow, and pressure.

solar energy—The photon energy originating from the sun's radiation in the wave length region from 0.3 to 2.7 micrometers.

solar factor—The mean daily solar radiation in langleys, divided by the heating degree days for the months of October through April.

solenoid valve—An electrically operated valve. When an electric current is applied to an electromagnet within the valve, a force is generated that causes the valve plunger to open or close.

specific heat—A measure of the amount of heat a material can hold for every degree its temperature is raised.

suitability index—The *solar factor* multiplied by the total heating bill in dollars for the October-through-April period. This provides a meaningful guideline as to the suitability of solar room heating in a specific geographic region.

therm—A unit of heat equal to 100,000 Btu. One therm equals 100 cu ft of natural gas.

Appendix B
Solar Manufacturers

The following list is not intended to include every solar manufacturer in business today, as there are literally hundreds of firms currently in existence. For a complete catalog, write:

ERDA Technical Information Center
Box 62
Oak Ridge, Tennessee

Ask for the catalog for *Solar Heating and Cooling Products*, document number ERDA-75.

Aluminum Company of America (Alcoa). Alcoa Building, Pittsburgh, Pennsylvania 15219. Manufacturer of swimming pool heaters.

Ametek. One Spring Ave., Hatfield, Pennsylvania 19440. Manufacturer of solar collectors and system design services.

Chamberlain Mfg. Corp. 845 Larch Ave., Elmhurst, Illinois 60126. Manufacturer of solar collectors.

Daystar Corp. 41 Second Ave., Burlington, Massachusetts 01803. Manufacturer of solar collectors.

Energex Corp. 5115 Industrial Road, Las Vegas, Nevada 89118. Manufacturer of solar collectors, water heaters, and swimming pool heaters.

Energy Systems, Inc. 634 Crest Drive, El Cajon, California. 92021. Manufacturer of solar collectors and complete systems.

Fafco, Inc. 138 Jefferson Drive, Menlo Park, California 94025. Manufacturer of swimming pool heaters.

Garden Way Laboratories. Box 66, Charlotte, Vermont 05445. Manufacturer of complete systems, solar collectors, water heaters, and system design services.

General Electric. Valley Forge Space Center, Box 8555, Philadelphia, Pennsylvania 19101. Manufacturer of solar collectors.

Grumman Aerospace Corp. Bethpage, New York 11714. Manufacturer of solar collectors, water heaters, and system design services.

Ilse Engineering, Inc. 7177 Arrowhead Road, Duluth, Minnesota 55811. Manufacturer of solar collectors.

InterTechnology Corp. 100 Main Street, Warrenton, Virginia 22186. Manufacturer of solar collectors.

Kalwall Corp. Box 237, Manchester, New Hampshire 03105. Manufacturer of solar collectors (air-type) and complete systems.

PPG Industries. One Gateway Center, Pittsburgh, Pennsylvania 15222. Manufacturer of solar collectors.

Raypac, Inc. 31111 Agoura Road, Westlake Village, California 91361. Manufacturer of swimming pool heaters.

Revere Copper and Brass. Box 151, Rome, New York 13440. Manufacturer of solar collectors.

Reynolds Metals Co. 6601 W. Broad St., Denver, Colorado 80022. Manufacturer of solar collectors.

Solaron Corp. 4850 Olive St. Denver, Colorado 80022. Manufacturer of complete systems (air-type) and system design services.

Sunsource. 9606 Santa Monica Blvd., Beverly Hills, California 92020. Manufacturer of water heaters.

Sunwater Company. 1112 Pioneer Way, El Cajon, California 92020. Manufacturer of water heaters.

Sunworks, Inc. 669 Boston Post Road, Guilford, Connecticut 06437. Manufacturer of solar collectors.

Thomason Solar Homes, Inc. 6802 Walker Mill Road, S.E., Washington, D.C. 20027. Manufacturer of solar collectors and complete systems.

Appendix C
Bibliography

For those of you who are interested in securing more information about solar energy, the following sources are provided. This is by no means a complete source of information, as more data is being released and more research is being done every day. But these are the sources I found useful in preparing this book, and I am sure they will be helpful to you.

Anderson, Lawrence B. *Santa Clara Community Center Project*. Lockheed Palo Alto Research Laboratory. Prepared for the American Institute of Aeronautics and Astronautics/American Astronomical Society, Solar Energy for Earth Conference, AAIA paper 75-608. Los Angeles, California. April 21—24, 1975.

Borzoni, J.T.; Holland, T.H.; and Ramsey, J.W. *Developement of Flat-Plate Solar Collectors for the Heating and Cooling of Buildings*. Honeywell Inc., Systems and Research Center, Minniapolis, Minnesota. Prepared for the National Aeronautics and Space Administration, NASA CR-134804. June 1975.

Catalog on Solar Energy Heating and Cooling Products. Energy Research and Development Administration, Division of Solar Energy. ERDA Technical Information Center, Oak Ridge, Tenn. October 1975.

Climatic Atlas of the United States. U.S. Department of Commerce. 1974.

Dempewolff, Richard F. *Sunpower: The Heat's On Oor Real*. Popular Mechanics. September 1975.

Diamond, Edward; Speiser, Kenneth. *The Energy House*. ASHRAE Journal. November 1975. Reprinted by Grumman Aerospace Corporation, Grumman Energy Programs, 2325-75. 1975.

Faltermayer, Edmund. *Solar Energy is Here, But It's Not Yet Utopia*. Fortune. February 1976.

Gordon, Harry. *Sugarmill Woods*. The Florida Architect. March 1975.

Hearings Before the Select Committee of Small Business, United States Senate, 94th Congress, parts 1, 1-A, 1-B, 1-C, 1-D, Appendices. U.S. Government Printing Office, Washington D.C. May 13, 1975.

Interim Performance Criteria for Commercial Solar Heating and Combined Heating/Cooling Systems and Facilities. National Aeronautics and Space Administration, George C. Marshall Space Flight Center, 98M10001. February 28, 1975.

Keyes, John. *Harnessing the Sun*, 2nd edition. Morgan & Morgan. Dobbs Ferry, New York. 1975.

Leckie, Jim; Masters, Gil; Whitehouse, Harry; Young, Lily. *Other Homes and Garbage.* Sierra Club Books. San Francisco, California. 1975.

Lior, N.; Saunders, A.P. *Solar Collector Performance Studies.* University of Pennsylvania. National Center for Energy Management and Power, Philadelphia, Pa. Prepared for the National Science Foundation, NSF-RA-N-74-152(3). 1974.

Lof, George O.G., et. al. *Design and Construction of a Residential Solar Heating and Cooling System.* Colorado State University, Solar Applications Energy Laboratory, Fort Collins, Colorado. Prepared for the National Science Foundation, NSF-RA-N-74-104. July 1974.

Low-Temperature Engineering Application of Solar Energy. ASHRAE members of technical committee on solar energy utilization, HS-5-75-1000. 1967.

Marchovich, Sharon J. *Autonomous Living in the Ouroboros House.* Popular Science. December 1975.

Melicher, Ronald W.; Sciglimpaglia, Donald M.; Scott, Jerome E. *Demand Analysis, Solar Heating and Cooling of Buildings—Solar Water Heating in South Florida: 1923—1974.* Phase I Report, prepared for the National Science Foundation, NSF-RA-N-74-190. December 1974.

Moore, Glenwood J., analyst. *Solar Energy Legislation Introduced in the 94th Congress.* Library of Congress, Science Policy Research Division. April 11, 1975.

Moore, Glenwood J.; Raliegh, Lani Hummel, analysts. *Survey of Solar Energy Products and Services.* Library of Congress, Science Policy Research Division. Prepared for the Subcommittee on Energy Research, Development, and Demonstration, 94th Congress (first session). June 1975.

Pullen, John J. *Energy from the Sun.* Country Journal. June 1975.

Residential Energy from the Sun. U.S. Department of Housing and Urban Development, Hud-402-PDR(2). July 1975.

Rittlemann, Richard P., architect. *The Atlanta School Project, Why Solar was Chosen and How the System Will Work.* Specifying Engineer. November 1975.

Santa Clara Community Recreation Center, Solar Heating and Cooling Project. City of Santa Clara, California. 1975.

Schlesinger, Robert J., P.E., president. Rho Sigma Inc. Personal communication, January 2, 1976.

Shurcliff, W.A. *Solar Heated Buildings, A Brief Survey,* 8th edition. 1975.

Solar Energy Applications. Papers presented to ASHRAE annual meeting, MO-74-1. June 23—27, 1974.

Solar Energy Engineering and Product Catalog. Rho Sigma Inc. Van Nuys, California.

Solar Energy School Heating Augmentation Experiment. InterTechnology Corp. Prepared for the National Science Foundation, NFS-RA-N-74-019. December 4, 1974.

Solar Energy Systems: the Practical Side. Architectural Record. August 1975.

Solar Energy Utilization for Heating and Cooling. ASHRAE Handbook and Product Directory, Applications Volume, Chapter 59. The American Society of Heating, Refrigerating, and Air Conditioning Engineers Inc. 1974.

Solar Heating and Cooling Experiment for a School in Atlanta. Westinghouse Electric Corporation, Special Systems, Baltimore, Maryland; Burt, Hill & Associates, Architects, Butler, Pa. NSF-C-908. December 1, 1974.

Solar Heating and Cooling of Buildings. General Electric. Phase 0, Feasibility and Planning Study, Vol. II, Final Report. Prepared for the National Science Foundation.   NSF-RA-N-74-021B. May 1974.

Solar Heating and Cooling of Buildings. TRW Systems Group, Redondo Beach, California. Phase 0, Volume II, Final Report. Prepared for the National Science Foundation, NSF-RA-N-74-022B. May 31, 1974.

Traver, Alfred E., PhD., P.E. *The Potential for Solar Heating and Cooling Residences in the State of Tennessee: Capture Analysis.* Tennessee Technical University, Cookeville, Tennessee. April 1975.

Index